21st Centur)

This might be news: success as a tw(
dependent on your technical aptitude al

As well as the basic requirements of understanding and applying the law superbly, you are also now expected to master a whole suite of so-called 'soft skills' – communicating empathetically, acting commercially, writing carefully, presenting brilliantly, networking sensibly and building relationships enthusiastically.

These skills might be called 'soft' by our industry, but the reality is that they are both incredibly hard and vitally important – especially as a junior commercial lawyer keen to make a likeable, professional, commercial and lasting positive impression on those in control of your embryonic career.

Written by a lawyer with unique experience as a commercial practitioner, trainer and law-firm voyeur, this no-nonsense 'how to' guide is an honest, punchy and modern look at all the skills you don't get taught at law school, yet are absolutely critical to achieving success from day one of your life as a twenty-first century solicitor.

Reviews

[A] tome of exceptional clarity ... Weiner's book is sensible and down-to-earth. Few would disagree with his premise – that to succeed, today's lawyer has to be more than merely technically proficient – and Weiner ably distils the ways that a junior lawyer can make a difference.

Alex Wade, The Times, Thursday December 15, 2011

An eye-opener for junior lawyers. A practical guide to the key business skills they need to develop. Highly recommended for any associate committed to their career.

Patrick McCann, Global Head of Learning and Development, Herbert Smith LLP

This book is a tool kit for all junior lawyers, written with a light touch but containing real substance, and covering all the key attributes for success as well as the potential pitfalls of life in practice. We have bought it for all our trainees.

Joanne Gubbay, Head of Practice Learning and Development, Ashurst LLP

There is no doubt in my mind that if you want to learn how to communicate effectively, increase your personal brand and commerciality to impress your colleagues, then you should take the time to read this book...While there is no manual, 21st Century Solicitor does a lot to bridge the gap so that paralegals, trainee solicitors and newly qualifieds can rest assured that not only are they making an impression, but that it is the right one and one that will be remembered for the right reasons. It is safe to say that this book is a must read for anyone working as a paralegal, trainee solicitor or newly qualified (and quite possibly could educate a few people who are already qualified).

The Law Society, Junior Lawyers Division

21st Century Solicitor

How to Make a Real Impact as a Junior Commercial Lawyer

Steve Weiner

·HART·
PUBLISHING

OXFORD AND PORTLAND, OREGON
2011

Published in the United Kingdom by Hart Publishing Ltd
16C Worcester Place, Oxford, OX1 2JW
Telephone: +44 (0)1865 517530
Fax: +44 (0)1865 510710
E-mail: mail@hartpub.co.uk
Website: http://www.hartpub.co.uk

Published in North America (US and Canada) by
Hart Publishing
c/o International Specialized Book Services
920 NE 58th Avenue, Suite 300
Portland, OR 97213-3786
USA
Tel: +1 503 287 3093 or toll-free: (1) 800 944 6190
Fax: +1 503 280 8832
E-mail: orders@isbs.com
Website: http://www.isbs.com

British Library Cataloguing in Publication Data
Data Available

ISBN: 978-1-84113-355-3

Typeset by Greg Sweetnam Design Solutions, Oxford
Printed and bound in Great Britain by
Lightning Source UK Ltd

Acknowledgements

I would like to thank the following people who helped to make this book possible:

Ann Collier for her time, her brilliant advice and her kind words;

Jo Gubbay for her support and encouragement in my transition from private practice to learning & development;

Richard Hart for believing in the book from the very start and making it happen;

Melanie Hamill and **Tom Adams** for their patience and hard work;

Alex Book for his creative contribution and friendship;

Simon McCall for his generosity and insight;

Shelley Weiner for her editorial input;

Jack Weiner and **Michelle Douek** for their love and support

Summary Contents

Contents

Introduction

A Modern Book for a Modern Solicitor?

This book is not like the other books — the books that repeat what marketing departments in law firms say, that churn out page after page of predictable theory or that give you 'practical' advice that is simply not relevant for you at your stage in your career. Those books are of little practical use to anyone. This book explores what it *actually* takes to be a successful 'starting out' lawyer in a corporate or commercial law firm.

WHO IS THIS BOOK FOR?

The focus is on the career of a solicitor, near the start of his or her career. The focus is on commercial or corporate law firms, since it was in these firms that I spent so much of my time as a professional, both as a lawyer and as a skills trainer and performance coach. This book is, in fact, the result of several thousands of hours of on-the-job research.

A little disclaimer ...

Please note that this book was not written with any specific law firm, lawyer, event or incident in mind. Nothing you read can be attributed to any lawyer, non-lawyer or firm unless expressed to be so. Rather, what follows is an examination of the **kinds of people** (lawyers and non-lawyers) and

situations you might come across in a commercial or corporate law firm, and how you might maximise your impact when you want to impress those in control (and even not in control) of your career. This book will not help you choose a specific firm to apply to or work in, but it will help prepare you for your first day at work.

Who are you?

If you are a trainee, you will need to know this stuff to qualify for the job you want. If you have recently qualified, you will need to know this stuff to maximise your chances of stepping up to the next level. If you are embarking on a career as a solicitor in a high-street firm and, having picked this book up, you are now thinking '*I won't need this, it's not relevant for me*', it is. Yes, there is a general commercial/corporate focus, but many of the themes covered in this book will help you succeed, regardless of which law firm you are in or are going to join.

WHY SHOULD YOU CARE?

It used to be the case that, not so very long ago, to succeed as a lawyer you simply needed to excel technically and the rest would take care of itself. Draft a memo on a brain-achingly complicated point of law, get your secretary to type it up, send it to the client and then hope for the best. Pray that the client doesn't call to talk it through with you. If he does, hope for the best and tell him about the law. Blind him with science.

How times have changed! The downturn in the economy has meant that people now expect more for less. Technology, which has revolutionised the way we do things, has also highlighted the failings of the two-fingered typing technique. But most importantly, **people** have changed. Now, doing 'the law' is the bare minimum. It is a minimum simply **expected** by those you need to impress, those being fellow lawyers, non-lawyers and clients.

Being bad at 'the law' as a lawyer is like a plumber coming round to your house to fix a leak only to tell you he '*doesn't do pipes*'. Ridiculous! Similarly, the lawyers you work with won't notice if you get the law right, only if you get it wrong. They won't care if 99 things you do are perfect; they will only care about the one thing you have done that is poor. So, it's fair to say that if you cannot get the law right (honest mistakes or lack of experience aside), you might as well give up, go home and watch daytime TV. Law may not be the career for you.

If, then, being a good technical lawyer is simply expected, how do you stand out and make a lasting impact? Well, when you are starting out, as well as the traditional legal-technical skills, you will now be expected to display competence in a whole range of what used to be called (erroneously) 'soft-skills'. These are things you probably think you are good at already — after all, surely, *it's all just common sense*? Whilst it might be 'common sense', however, that does not mean it will be 'common practice'.

The reason for this shift in expectation? Times are changing. Where people once named fish and chips as their favourite take-away, nowadays it is much more likely to be sushi. Where families once holidayed in a campervan in Bognor Regis, they are now more likely to jump on the Eurostar after work and head off to Paris for a quick city-break. And where actually having a lunch break at work used to mean a trip to the local wine bar, it is now more likely to involve a spinning class at the local health and fitness centre.

Similarly, partners of law firms no longer enjoy plush offices with lavish, mahogany drinks cabinets, neither do they conclude deals over a round of golf after lunch. These days, in fact, they will readily use phrases such as *'let's sit down and discuss this in the coffee area'*, *'I want to make sure we give the client exactly what they want!'* and *'is everyone happy with what they are doing?'* in team meetings whilst drinking an organic smoothie. Most importantly, things have become a whole lot more **people-** and **team-oriented**.

Coupled with this, business is more sophisticated. Clients demand more from their legal advisers. New commercial and legal risks have emerged, requiring lawyers to adapt accordingly to win the best clients and the best work. Most importantly for you, lawyers are no longer chosen as a sole result of the documents they produce or the technical advice they give. Clients decide between law firms on the basis of the people they provide, and because of the personalities they have. And similarly, your success as a junior lawyer depends on whether or not you 'fit in', 'stand out' and get on with the individuals who might shape your progress.

Don't forget that law firms are a uniquely bizarre and eclectic mixture of old-fashioned values and practices coupled with twenty-first-century business and skills trends. They are an awkward, evolving melting-pot of belief systems, egos, habits and intellectual pursuits. As a 'bright young thing' coming into the profession, you are perfectly positioned to make an impact that will maximise your opportunity for long-term success. To do so, you have to follow certain rules and accepted models, pushing behavioural boundaries and taking a few calculated behavioural 'risks' to reflect the changing nature of the expectations placed on you by those who are in control of your career.

Within law firms, partners and senior lawyers now expect more people and 'business' skills to be displayed by their juniors (despite the fact that they might lack the skills themselves). They want junior lawyers they would be happy to put in front of an important client without worrying about them saying or doing the wrong thing.

Don't forget that the profession is increasingly heavily regulated, more competitive, more globalised in its reach, more complex in terms of the work undertaken and increasingly reliant on the ability of its lawyers to 'sell' their service.

At your level, selling your service is simply about impressing your peers and your colleagues. Once you have done that, you will be given your chance to sell yourself to clients externally. The second won't happen until you have proved you can do the first. It is about doing the law well and doing the other skills even better — skills that are far from soft, skills that are as hard as it gets.

With all this in mind, this book will focus only on the things you might need to do to **stand out**, **make an impact** and **sell yourself** as a junior commercial lawyer. It will not tell you how to do the law, to record time effectively, to draft documents, to undertake research or conduct a due diligence project. **This is not a technical legal handbook.** Rather, this book will examine what impactful junior lawyers do. Eighty per cent of it is about communication skills in some form, and the remaining 20 per cent is about cultivating and displaying an active and visible interest in the things you do (ie business!). You will learn a lot from those around you as you progress through your early career, but this book will give you the tools to hit the ground running[1] — or at least walking briskly — when you start out and until you get to grips with things.

In food terms, this book aims to take you from baked potato with cheese and beans (solid, comforting and enjoyable, but predictable, unexciting, unremarkable and easily outdone) to baked fillet of Black Cod with a herb crust, a sweet potato and parmesan mash, and a medley of honey-glazed seasonal vegetables with a pea and mint purée (multi-faceted, exciting, fresh, delicious, innovative, exclusive and highly sought-after).

Please note that in contrast with much of the literature on this subject, the writer of this book solemnly **promises** and **undertakes** to:

- make this book interesting (as far as possible ...)

- be honest

- make things as useful and practical as possible, but without stating the obvious

- make this book an appropriate length — not too long and not too short.

---

[1] Apologies for the use of this terrible phrase. Sadly, you might hear a lot of it over the next few years ...

A warning ...

This is a manual — not an encyclopaedia, a bible or a roadmap for guaranteed success as a professional. This book is not intended as a blueprint for the rest of your career; it just explains how to make an impact at the start when you don't really know how to do that. After all, you can't become a partner in one year, but you can destroy any chances of becoming a partner in a firm within a matter of six months (or less!).

This book is a good starting point for you, but is not intended to be any more than that. You will find your own style and a way to act around others that works for you in time. Then you can kick on in a way that suits you when it feels right and put this book on your bookshelf to be handed down to the next generation of young, keen commercial lawyers.

YES, BUT WILL IT BE PRACTICAL?

This book should be of tangible, practical use to you — the reader and junior legal practitioner. Many books you might read in the areas I intend to cover will tell you, for example, to 'be confident' or 'act assertively', without telling you how this might practically be achieved and in what situations this might be appropriate. For you, this approach is frustrating, irritating and mildly patronising — like paying a fitness instructor who tells you at the start of each session to 'get fitter', then proceeds to run aimlessly around a park for an hour asking you to follow him before demanding payment. You'd feel cheated, frustrated and probably a little bit angry.

Here, where relevant and appropriate, you will be provided with strategies, formulae and particularised action plans, structuring theory and advice — where relevant and appropriate — around practical methodology.

Obviously, this will not work for every section of this book, and there will be some chapters where the focus is on behavioural issues that are intrinsically 'softer' in their scope. However, if you do need to do something or act in a specific way in any given situation, suggestions will be made as to how you might approach it.

With all this in mind, please read this book if:

- You are curious about what exactly it is that successful lawyers are like and do.

- You are thinking about becoming a lawyer, in a very speculative, *'I've got a good degree from a good university'* kind of way, but have no real understanding of the job spec.

- You are a trainee solicitor.

- You are intending to qualify as a commercial lawyer quite soon.

- You are practising as a junior lawyer.

- You are supervising or mentoring a junior lawyer in a commercial law firm.

- You can laugh at yourself.

- You have just been made redundant and need something to do.

1

Why People Become Lawyers

This book is about making a lasting and positive impact as a junior commercial lawyer. A huge part of that lies in understanding that everyone has a 'brand' at work. This brand may be excellent, average or poor. We shall look at what a successful junior commercial lawyer's brand might comprise in chapter three.

Before that, it might be helpful to consider the wider commercial or corporate law brand. What attracts people to corporate or commercial legal practice? Why do people choose to become commercial lawyers in the first place? It might not be something you think about much, but once you can identify and understand your true underlying motivations for choosing the profession, it becomes much easier to exploit them to optimum effect and avoid the many potential pitfalls that will inevitably come your way in practice.

WHAT MOTIVATES INDIVIDUALS TO BECOME LAWYERS?

Television shows

Television shows such as *LA Law* or *Ally McBeal* might make you believe that everyone in a law firm is available and attractive, there are unisex toilets on every floor, that you will always inhabit spacious offices with skyline views, that double-breasted suits are cool and that you will have loads of time to spend your fat pay packet in swanky bars where the opposite sex finds your intellectual swagger irresistible. Wake up and smell the compromise agreement! Expect this and you *will* be disappointed.

The money

Being a high-earning lawyer is a lifestyle choice. But be under no illusions. You will not have a great social life if you earn a lot (or even quite a lot) of money being a lawyer. As one partner said, '*I don't make arrangements during the week as I just know I'll just have to cancel them!*' The phrase '*We might have to come in Saturday morning*' is a law firm euphemism for '*You will definitely have to work all weekend*'.

Although these are exaggerations and by no means the norm, be clear — this is no nine-to-five job. It is a lifestyle choice, much like being a doctor. Most lawyers do not know that there is a TV programme called *The One Show*, let alone ever get home in time to see it. Rarely will they be home in time for *Holby City* (every cloud ... !). However, the intellectual rewards can be huge if you give it your all. But all means *all*. In saying this, many forget that it is *still* a job. And those lawyers who retain perspective are invariably the most successful and inspirational ones.

The glamour

Being a solicitor is a great job. However, contrary to popular belief, there is little that is overly glamorous about the role. While running high-profile meetings in plush offices might be quite exciting, and going along to a completion dinner in the London 'Gherkin' might be a bit 'red carpet', most people agree that working until 10pm every night for a month and a half to 'float' a company is not glamorous. It is just exhausting.

THE HIGH-PROFILE WORK

High-profile' or 'quality' work is another tricky concept. You might work for a huge, 'sexy' multi-national that has just floated for squillions on the FTSE. And the work will challenge you intellectually…eventually. As a trainee or newly-qualified solicitor, however, you will have to earn your stripes proofreading, photocopying, bundling, low-level drafting and preparing research notes that might not be used or paid for. This can be frustrating. It is, however, the only way to get ahead and prove to those around you that you have what it takes. This 'rite of passage' is not unique to just the legal industry.

FACING THE REALITY

If you are joining a medium to large commercial or corporate law firm (by which we mean one that has some kind of corporate, commercial, finance, real estate and (probably) litigation departments), the main thing that matters is money. Money, money, money. It is the rich man's world. Money makes the world go round. And it makes your law firm go round as well. Ultimately, it also makes the partners become rounder.

Your clients are business people. They want to make money. They don't like the law – it stops them from having fun and restricts their ability to conduct their business. That is why they pay lawyers to help them do what they want to do in their chosen commercial field. If you fail to understand their commercial goals, you are stuffed. You will be targeted in the next round of redundancies. Or worse, you will turn into what people politely call a *'legal eagle'*. This is not a compliment.

'But why?' you might think to yourself, *'I was trained to interpret, uphold and apply the law? Surely it is about apportioning my clients' risks? Surely money is the secondary by-product of my vocation in life?'*

That is all perfectly correct, but if you think only like that and not like a business person, you won't achieve success. Remember, a modern lawyer is a salesman. They sell their legal knowledge and advice to business people who need to trust them as commercial and not just legal advisors. After all, people buy people. People do not buy law. Law is, on the whole, boring to everyone who is not a lawyer. To be successful, therefore, you have to sell a business approach to applying the law.

Combined with this, business people do not generally enjoy working with others who are:

- arrogant

- patronising

- uninterested

- boring or obviously bored

- lacking in commercial 'acumen'

- easily offended

- humourless.

'That's obvious!' you may be thinking. It might be when you read it in a book. When you start work in a law firm, however, you might not notice when you start becoming the very person you do not like and/or laugh at. This is because there is a slight risk that your ego might take over. Remember that you have spent most of your life being gifted or clever. People have probably told you so for years. You might well be popular, and you might even think you are brilliant and interesting. Nevertheless, it may be time to re-install your factory settings and take note of the following:

- The fact that you are 'clever' or 'bright', have an IQ of 243 and probably went to a good university (being the type where you '**read**' Law, or perhaps History, Philosophy, English or Classics, as opposed to one in which you '**did**' Law) is of no significance. It is the romantic equivalent of telling someone on a date that your mum thinks you are good-looking or beautiful. It means nothing and is a total turn-off. Trainee or newly-qualified, you are now at the bottom of the food chain in a very large pond.

- You will need to decide pretty quickly what kind of solicitor (and person) you want to become. You will then need to stick to your guns. Career aside, the last thing you want is to become that person friends describe as having 'gone weird' after starting work. 'Weird' means horrific. To avoid this there are a few skills you will have to get to grips with, and a number of lessons you will need to learn.

If you understand the above, whatever your route into law, you are at a very exciting stage of your career. Working in commercial law firms can be challenging and stressful, but the benefits and rewards on every level are huge – if you get your mindset and thought processes organised correctly early on.

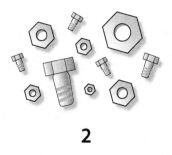

2

The Basics

An integral part of being a successful lawyer is about making an impact intellectually: drafting water-tight documents, making incisive legal-technical observations, giving succinct, correct advice and being 100 per cent technically accurate.

However, it's worth remembering the following:

a) Your brilliant legal-technical brain will count for nothing in profitability terms if you cannot communicate your brilliance and build relationships with those you work with and for.

b) Your clients will not pay your bills if you have not shown them that you care about their business, their business needs and/or their strategic goals.

You will come across many lawyers (especially in transactional practice areas) who not only will display a brilliant legal-technical talent or aptitude when they need to, but also will display a real talent for people skills. They always seem to have time to chat, they spend a lot of time engaged in business development activities, they show an appropriate interest in everything at work, they are generally popular and they smile a lot (oh, and they deliver cracking advice too ...). These are the lawyers you need to emulate.

DOING THE BASICS ...

Charge-out rates and salary aside, it may feel as though there is very little difference between being a final-seat trainee and a newly-qualified (NQ) or junior solicitor. For the first year after qualification, NQs might feel like they are flying by the seat of their pants. And an NQ's instinct will simply be to get to grips with the technical stuff and to try to vindicate the firm's decision to invest in him or her as a professional. Unlike when the NQ was a trainee, as time passes very few colleagues will volunteer to spend time formally evaluating an NQ's progress. Formal feedback aside, the NQ will largely be left to sink or swim, whatever Human Resources (HR) might say. If he or she sinks, the NQ might be jettisoned quickly and might never make it to two years' post-qualification experience (PQE). If he or she swims, however, the NQ will not be jettisoned —yet.

So, if you are swimming, what makes the difference between success and failure? Following the aquatic analogy, consider the three 'swimmers' below:

Dillip — swims very fast but looks awful and always forgets to breathe; he wins most races but nearly dies doing so.

Anya — swims neatly and always at a reliably medium pace, with her head out of the water (so her hair does not get wet) despite being under 60. This is most irritating to watch, for all concerned. Anya struggles to swim fast, even in a race.

Chris — swims with a near-perfect and very professional-looking technique, and has a thirst for improvement. Chris is solid and rarely ruffled in a race. He can swim fast but is sometimes slow, and ocassionally loses races.

Extending this analogy to the legal profession, which 'swimmer' would be the most successful solicitor? In deciding, you should understand that when considering whether or not to retain faith in you, those in charge of your career want to see if you:

a) train all the time, never taking time to reflect and simply tread water in terms of progress, turning into a one dimensional swimming-drone like Dillip or display an inability to adapt to the circumstances, irritatingly plodding along like Anya ; or

b) train regularly and enthusiastically but not manically, become a safe swimmer with a rock-solid technique and an ability to adapt to the needs of the race, learning from losses, and at the same time display your enjoyment for everything you do and a perceived hunger for improvement, like Chris.

If you fall into category a), you will struggle; if you fall into category b), you are on the road to success. No one in charge of your career really expects you to swim very fast, very quickly all the time from day one. On the whole, you should swim quite slowly (unless speed is needed or requested), swim **pretty**, make minimum splash and ignore what others around you at your level are doing to focus on your own improvement.

What does 'pretty' mean? It means making people think you are in control when in reality you sometimes might not be. Of course you will have to work very hard, and sometimes you will have to chuck yourself in and give it a go (understanding your limitations and seeking help where appropriate). The rest is about maximising your visibility, building relationships, showing everyone you 'care' for every element of the job and doing the basics well. Then you begin to make yourself integral to your team and, eventually, vital to the law firm's business. That is when you move on to more complex matters, more intellectually challenging work and deeper levels of trust with those who control your career and those external to the organisation. Which is a great place to be.

BUT HOW IS YOUR SUCCESS MEASURED?

We have mentioned 'swimming pretty', but success is also about money. Cold, hard money. You might be the right 'kind' of person to become a solicitor, but if you don't make money for your firm, you can forget about being successful. To that extent, working in a professional services organisation is first and foremost about billing – or billing enough. To extend the swimming analogy, if you swim pretty but fail to wear a swimming costume, people will quickly notice — and probably not for the right reasons.

Billing enough time, like wearing swimming trunks, is simply expected. It is not a differentiator. In branding speak, it is simply a 'hygiene' factor. Meeting or exceeding chargeable time targets, recording time properly, reducing the amount of time spent sitting on files ('Work in Progress' or 'WIP') by sending out bills quickly, improving cash-flow and getting clients to pay as soon as possible, all are vital for profitability. And whilst you probably won't be responsible for managing external client relationships or billing and fee arrangements with these clients as a junior, you will be expected to do your bit to ensure such profitability as soon as you qualify as a commercial lawyer, and even as a trainee. What 'your bit' is will be communicated to you in no uncertain terms at the appropriate time. Each firm will have a different policy — your job is to keep up. Fall behind and others will notice very quickly.

Having said that, if you are just a billing lawyer (ie a legal plodder — a non client-facing, backroom, document production specialist), your firm might focus simply on the deficit in your hours at appraisal time. The fact that you have worked every weekend since January will not come into the equation. The powers that be probably won't congratulate you for the extra hours because no one will really see you doing them (and if they do, they will keep quiet about it for fear of looking average themselves).

The situation may be worse still if you spend hour upon hour in the office yet fail to record them all. You will still get into trouble when your 'utilisation' (a term law firms use to denote being busy with stuff that will make the business money) goes down and others' figures stay healthy.

The point to note is that the expectation to bill **enough** never ever goes away. However, it does not need to be as stark as this. Yes, you will have to record enough time and, yes, sometimes you will have to stay late and work very hard through the night. But provided you make the right impact, cultivate a positive personal brand and show an aptitude for a range of non legal-technical skills, the importance and visibility of your utilisation will reduce. You may even get away with not achieving anything like your chargeable target. And when you tell your boss that you have to leave this evening at 18:30 to meet friends, he will say *'Have a good evening, thanks for all your work over the past few days,'* rather than *'Oh, can you just help me with something before you go?'*

In other words, you can go the extra mile without doing anything extra.

3

Personal Brand and Lawyers

Making a lasting, positive impact as a junior lawyer is hard. The key to a positive impact lies in owning a strong, positive personal brand. Communicating such a brand to those you work with and for from day one of your career as a junior commercial lawyer is absolutely vital. This is because successful business people both understand and perpetuate their own positive personal brand.

PERSONAL BRAND AND YOU

Everyone, from the man who owns and runs your local corner shop to the CEO of a FTSE-index listed company has a 'personal brand'. The people who do best are the ones who manage their brand for maximum impact. Some people have no idea how to do this. Others are brilliant at it. At the start of your career, you will probably fall into the first bracket. So, putting the fancy marketing jargon aside, what exactly is 'personal brand'?

For our purposes personal brand comprises two simple elements:

1) **How you view and portray yourself** — when you think of yourself, what do **you believe** is true?

2) **How others view you and the way you portray yourself** — when **others** think of you, what pops into their heads?

At work, it is only really element (2) that matters. In other words, the reality is what others see and think of you. It does not matter what you think of yourself; it is what others think of you that counts. Personal brand 'nirvana' exists where elements (1) and (2) coincide. In other words, when others see and hear exactly what you want them to see and hear — no more and no less. How do you achieve this? It's about consistently exploring your own brand to increase self-awareness and project effectively what you want others to see. This sounds simple but it's not — especially when you are starting out.

What is Personal Brand?

When people think of brands, words like 'Apple', 'Nike', 'Coca-Cola' or 'Honda' usually spring to mind. But what about words like 'America', 'London', 'Christianity', 'Capitalism', 'Obama' or 'Beckham'? What about words that refer to things that don't even exist: 'Mickey Mouse'? What these words all have in common is that their mere mention sparks a series of ideas, images and impressions in your mind — and the mind of anyone else who has ever come into contact with the relevant subject. Ultimately, that is all that is required for the existence of a 'brand'. When people who know you hear or read your name, the same thing happens; if all these things are brands, then so is 'You'.

A brand is not a logo, or a name, or a look — it probably uses some kind of 'visual identity' to ensure consistency, but that is certainly not what defines it. Brand is 'The collective perception of a company, place, object, concept, group or individual'.

So the definition of your personal brand is 'The collective perception of you'. The critical element in this is realising that what matters is not how you want to be perceived, but how you are perceived. In a perfect world these two things are one and the same, but in reality that is almost never the case. In other words, brands are not created in the marketing departments or boardrooms of big global corporations, they are created in the minds of the people who interact with them. The image IS the brand — what we are talking about here is reputation.

What this means is that everyone could be said to have a 'brand', whether they like it or not. The question is, now you know that it exists, how can you ensure it reflects you in the most desirable light? Of the names listed above, some are acutely aware of their brand and work consciously on building and supporting it; others are more passive and allow their reputation to speak for itself. Both approaches have merits —in many respects the ideal position is to be the former, but be perceived as the latter — but in all likelihood the most appropriate option for you will be somewhere in between. Self-awareness is critical, but even in the most professional and driven of workplaces it remains important to be human.

The most important starting point is knowing that the most successful brands don't lie about what they are — they don't have to. Their brands are built around their true values and capabilities and require no polishing to be appealing. In the same way, successful personal brand management is about identifying the most important and engaging elements within you and understanding how to bring them to the fore. Marketing and branding fails when it is nothing more than a pretty idea with no substance beneath. In other words, don't just make up 'the perfect personal brand' and try to modify yourself to fit; instead, aim to create a brand that truly represents and amplifies who you really are.

It is only once you have thought carefully — and honestly — about your ambitions, your values and your capabilities, that you can move on to working out how to focus your everyday actions and behaviours such that 'the collective perception of you' can gradually align with where you want it to be: a genuine amplification of the very best of your attitudes, abilities, beliefs and character.

Alex Book, Senior Brand Consultant, MEAT Global Brand Consultancy

DO AS I SAY, NOT AS I DO...

If the best business people and lawyers are self-aware and in charge of their own brands, how is it that some old-school lawyers (and non-lawyers) many might think of as 'successful' have such terrible brands and do not seem to care?

When many of these individuals were training as lawyers or working in law firms, being a 'people person' was not high on the list of priorities. In fact, little tangible value was attached to being liked, and no one really cared if you were interested in treating others as you like to be treated. Often, firms were known for being male-dominated and having a rather sexist and ruthlessly aggressive approach to business. And if you were practising in a firm like this, being a technical lawyer was all you needed to prove your competency and credibility as a professional.

Because of this, when you are observing certain individuals at work, you need to do as they **say**, not as they **do**. For example, a lawyer might tell you that treating your secretary well is vital to your success as a junior, only to bark orders at that same secretary without so much as a please or thank you. This is a symptom of having a serious lack of self-awareness. That lawyer might know what to say and how to act when pushed (HR told them so), but he or she might not really believe in it. You must not be like this.

How might you prove yourself to these people? It used to be norm that working in a commercial law firm – or any law firm for that matter — as a junior lawyer meant that you were expected to suffer to earn your stripes. You would be legitimately and casually scolded by your seniors, learning by passive-aggressive 'osmosis' as you sequenced through your torturous training.

Of course, you might still see some terrible behaviour from senior colleagues. And to impress them, you might have to occassionally just suck it up to get the job done well. However, things are evolving. Being treated well in the workplace is now a key ingredient for organisational success, including in law firms. That isn't to say that everyone is nice all the time. There are times when urgency dictates that senior colleagues simply need to tell rather than ask. However, the best lawyers and role-models use an iron fist in a velvet glove to get things done, always remaining aware of their brand to ensure it is not damaged. Similarly, you need to be conscious of how you might be coming across to others who might not be as stressed as you. If you can master this skill early on, you have a great opportunity to carve a niche for yourself.

The truth is, senior lawyers are getting younger. People are reaching partnership at an earlier age. The dinosaurs are on their way out. The new, successful, shiny and aspirational twenty-first-century partner will be the kind of lawyer who might hold 'brainstorming' sessions to get input from others before making a decision, who will ask searching questions rather than dictate instructions, who might prefer face-to-face communication to e-mail, deliver trainee and even client training sessions without making a fuss, who will substantively engage with the appraisal process and use words and phrases like *'cool'*, *'let's understand the **commercial drivers** here'* and *'how do you **feel** about that?'*. They are genuinely interested in other people and how those people view them, proactively and assertively managing this perception in numerous ways. Their example should be followed as you sequence through your career.

THE MEANING OF SELF-AWARENESS

Being self-aware is about understanding the context in which you work. It is appreciating that the basic rules of decent human interaction (plus some tailored specifically to work) are perfectly applicable in a law firm. Interactions in a professional context are still human interactions. It follows, therefore, that building rapport, common courtesy, basic politeness, assertiveness, humility, levity and empathy are all crucial if you are to own a successful personal brand.

And good humour. People like people who laugh at themselves (appropriately). Generally speaking, in a high-pressured business environment, good humour and (reasonable) self-deprecation are valuable behavioural assets. Good humour does not mean telling jokes, being witty and being the 'life and soul'. That quickly becomes tiring and irritating. Equally, self-deprecation does not mean ridiculing oneself in front of people you need to impress ('*What would I know? I'm just a trainee/ an NQ!*'). The point is to recognise that it is important to enjoy what you are doing whilst appreciating the need to take it very seriously.

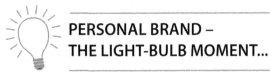

PERSONAL BRAND – THE LIGHT-BULB MOMENT...

Managing brand is all about perspective, understanding the context in which you work and appropriate behaviour modification where necessary. You should be questioning your behaviour all the time, and especially before key events. Questions like:

- Are extremes of emotion appropriate in this instance?

- How might the phrase '*I don't understand*' come across to others?

- What will they think of me if I raise my voice?

- What will they think of me if I do not turn up to that training session?

- Do I need to say thank you every time I ask my secretary to do something for me?

- Is sending an e-mail the best way to deliver good or bad news?

- Did I talk down to them when I told them they had made a mistake?

- I know I do not feel stressed, but do I need to display a sense of urgency to please partner X who always appears to be stressed?

One thing you should not do is to worry about this. That will have a detrimental effect on your brand. You run the risk of coming across as unnatural and neurotic. Much of this behaviour will develop organically. Whilst you might be thinking to yourself:

- This is the first time I have worked seriously in a law firm (or anywhere properly) and it's terrifying!

- Will just being myself work for me in my chosen law firm?

- How do I strike the right balance between being a nice, congenial person and a successful, ambitious person? In other words, how do I avoid adding weight to the 'nice guys come last' theory?

- Surely I need to show that I am good at the law before I can concentrate on the other things?

These concerns shouldn't engulf your thought-processes. Whilst they are all valid considerations, to ensure they do not affect your behaviour in a negative way you simply need to keep an eye on your external brand as much as you can — day-to-day, month-to-month and year-to-year — to strike a balance between 'you' and 'you at work'. This means maintaining an ongoing interest in regular self-reflection and appraisal, and always asking yourself before key interactions and events, '*Is this a personal brand moment?*'.

THE MODEL?

In branding yourself as an excellent junior lawyer, you might want to think in terms of the three facets displayed in Figure 3.1 below.

Figure 3.1   *Balancing the facets of your brand*

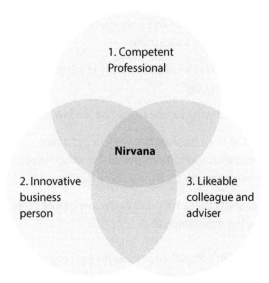

The best young lawyers straddle all three elements in Figure 3.1 to occupy personal brand nirvana. They are respected by clients (internal and external alike), they think strategically and advise on matters that are not strictly law-related, they are aware of their own limitations, they are popular (because they are self-aware and are genuinely interested in others around them) and they don't work 24/7.

Further, no matter how stressed they are, they always have time for others (either now or at an agreed time later on) they are approachable, calm and good-natured. They are also great communicators. They show empathy, understanding, they listen carefully and react accordingly, they never show aggression and they are appropriately enthusiastic about every element of their job – even the rubbish bits.

TIME TO BED IN?

From day one you will be expected to display the requisite legal-technical competence. Although people will expect you to make mistakes, how you deal with those mistakes is what will set you apart. Specifically, how you deliver work and deal with difficult situations as a junior lawyer will be examined from the word 'go', as people ask:

- Do they get defensive when given critical feedback, or do they seem grateful and energetic in developing themselves?

- Are they proactive or neurotic in seeking and absorbing feedback?

- Do they display a relevant sense of calm when appropriate?

- Are they in control of their emotions?

- Are they able to give me exactly what I want when I want it?

- Do they ask the right questions when we work together?

- Are they and do they look organised and well-drilled?

- Can they turn on the charm and communicate appropriately?

At the sharp end of the stick, how you handle yourself in high-pressure situations will contribute significantly to your brand early on in your career. In those 'crunch' situations, how do you manage? Is your stress out there for everyone to see? Do you 'lose it'? Do you reveal a new side to your personality that you perhaps should have kept under wraps?

Starting out

How do you know if you are entering negative personal brand territory? How do you know whether others think you are too fragile, assertive or relaxed? You ask. Procuring and receiving feedback is a vital part of researching and establishing your brand at the start. Why? Because asking for feedback shows:

a) you are interested in developing yourself; and

b) you care what others think; and

c) you don't take yourself too seriously; and

d) you are a team player.

You will receive feedback from obvious sources (like partners, senior lawyers and other legally-qualified colleagues) as well as from less obvious ones (eg your secretary, business services or support staff like training and development advisers, your accounts team and others). The important thing is that you accept all feedback gratefully and show that you have incorporated appropriate suggestions for improvement into your day-to-day conduct, no matter how small. Remember that some people are more receptive to/better at giving feedback than others. Always consider this before asking.

There is a fine line between proactively asking for regular feedback and altering behaviour accordingly, and displaying neurotic under-confidence by worrying 24/7. How do you strike the right balance? Some ideas are set out in Table 3.1 below.

Table 3.1 *Asking for and utilising feedback*

I get feedback by ...	Proactive and confident or neurotic and needy?
Asking my supervisor or the supervising partner after completing each new piece of work	It is not appropriate to get feedback on every new piece of work you do. Only on the significant and challenging new tasks.
Asking my supervisor or the supervising partner after completing a challenging, new piece of work but when the matter or deal has completed	A good idea. Ask in person when it might be convenient to get some feedback on your performance (both technically and as a team member), and then use Outlook to put something in the diary to discuss at a mutually convenient time.

Asking my supervisor or the supervising partner at the end of a deal or matter	There is nothing wrong with asking for a quick catch-up on your general performance over the course of a deal or matter. Make it quick and snappy; no more than 15 minutes.
Asking the person with whom I worked most closely at the end of a deal or matter	This is vital. Do not assume that only the senior lawyers with whom you worked will give you valuable feedback. You will get some really useful input from junior colleagues as well as mid-ranking associates who spent time with you (often when you were most stressed) throughout the matter. Did you work with non-lawyers? Perhaps catch up with them over a coffee to discuss how it went. Do not make the mistake of always going back to the same person for advice and feedback. You run the risk of being perceived as irritating.
Setting up two-monthly review meetings (for 30 minutes) with my direct supervisor, bringing copies of all challenging work completed by me to discuss	A sensible idea, time-permitting. Keep a file of all feedback received from all sources, and present this to your direct supervisor every two months and ask if there is anything he or she would like to add. Keep this file up-to-date. It will come in very handy at appraisal/review time.

I get feedback by ...	Proactive and confident or neurotic and needy?
Taking my secretary out for coffee or lunch once every month/three weeks and asking him/her if there is anything I can improve in the way we work together	A bare minimum. Be flexible on timings and alert to your secretary's workload. Simply taking your secretary for coffee or lunch (even to a canteen) to ask if there is anything you might do to make his/her life easier at work is a great source of feedback and a fantastic way to pre-empt rumour-mongering and gossip. Do not go anywhere too flash, but always pay. Doing this also shows real sensitivity.
Adding the question 'Is that ok' after each piece of work I give to my secretary	No! This screams under-confidence and a 'wet' approach to delegation. If your secretary has a problem, he/she will tell you. Save it for the aforementioned catch-up lunch! Be assertive and clear. Always ask if there are any questions at the end, and make enough time to delegate effectively. Don't shoehorn 15 minutes into 5!
Sometimes asking the question 'What would make things easier/easiest for you?' when giving work to business service or support staff	Use this when working on complicated matters and/or issues. Remember, all feedback is good feedback! Make sure you also show an interest in making life as easy as possible for those you work with in the support functions. Use phrases like 'I am sure you are really busy but ...' and 'How can I help you get this done?' and 'Is there any way I can do things differently next time to make things easier for you?'

A top personal philosophy when you are starting out

To enhance your chances of owning a successful brand when you are starting out as a solicitor, you should regard the term 'client' as referring to anyone you come across in a professional capacity. In other words, when you start life as a solicitor, you should aim to treat everyone you come across at work (from the Reprographics Assistant to the Managing Partner) as if they were CEO of one of the firm's most important clients – within reason. Remember, reputations are built over a life-time and destroyed in the short time it takes for you to say *'What's wrong with you?! I explained this already!'.*

Think of yourself as a public company, with everything you do at work affecting the value of your 'shares' and how much others might want to invest in you (or, in the law firm context, work with you as a professional). Every action/inaction at work will have a direct impact on that share price. As such, you can alter your performance to increase your share value.

Most of all, be interested in your own development. Modify your behaviour when you need to. Start with small but highly-visible changes, and as you get more experienced incorporate bigger behavioural shifts. Before every professional interaction, consider how your behaviour is going to affect the way others perceive you. Never rush into anything as a lawyer, and never react to anything you experience out of raw emotion. Step back and take stock. Then move to action.

Crucially, plan and own everything you do, and always have time for everyone, no matter how senior or junior (if not now, then at a suitable time later on). And every time you think something is common **sense**, ask yourself whether it is common **practice**. Is it so obvious that you are not doing it?

4

Be Empathetic – Communication Skills for Maximum Impact

COMMUNICATION AND BRAND

The best twenty-first-century solicitors are great communicators. Of that there is no doubt. They communicate positively, clearly, enthusiastically, likeably, commercially and insightfully with colleagues, peers, supervisors, mentors and clients alike. Communicating effectively and efficiently is key to your success as a junior commercial lawyer.

The truth is, being a great communicator is not rocket science. In simple terms, it is about making the effort to communicate with others in the way they want to be communicated with. Becoming proficient in this is most important when you are starting out, because it will be you, and not others, who will need to adapt and tailor your approach to suit the styles of others — others who might control the direction of your career (internally and externally). Adapt and tailor effectively, and they will notice subconsciously when you get it right. You will be rewarded with big brownie points.

WHAT SKILLS ARE WE THINKING ABOUT?

The term 'skills' is applied perhaps most tangibly in the field of communication. Communication is at the heart of a successful outward brand because it is what everyone notices every day at work all the time, irrespective of background. You will be judged according to how you communicate in every facet of your working life. This will form a huge part of others' 'perception' of you. Of course, less sophisticated communicators might not notice as much. However, you don't need to be a genius to observe that someone is acting aggressively, or that he's a push-over in an argument or discussion, or that he makes a funny squeaking noise when he cries — and that he cries a lot.

So, what are we talking about when we say *X is a wonderful communicator*? Some might argue that being a great communicator is the same as being a great public speaker. Some elements are certainly common to both. It would be wrong, however, to assume that they are the same thing. After all, if you were to watch certain stand-up comics performing in front of and communicating with complete strangers so confidently on stage, you might assume they were great communicators off-stage as well. More likely is that your average stand-up comic is a profoundly inept communicator – great in front of a crowd but terrible when faced with a situation calling for intimate, interpersonal communication. Comics are proof indeed that one does not equal the other.

Most lawyers, however, are not performers (although some might delude themselves that they are stand-up comics ...). Given the advisory nature of the job, effective one-to-one, interpersonal (rather than group) communication is key to maximising impact and personal brand at work in a law firm. It is what you should focus on. Of course, competent and engaging public speaking, and insightful, engaging presentation skills are important weapons to have in your arsenal as a junior commercial lawyer. However, they are a different beast entirely, and something we will examine in chapter six.

WHAT, THEN, IS A GREAT COMMUNICATOR?

Dr Albert Mehrabian, a communication guru from the United States, spent a lot of time looking at what the elements of effective communication might be. He believed effective communication revolved around understanding and mastering three key areas:

a) **What we say**, ie the words and language we use;

b) **How we say it**, ie the tone, pace, intonation and expression in our voice when we speak;

c) **What we look like when we say it**, ie the non-verbal signals (what your hands are doing, how you stand or sit, what you do with your eyes and your smile, fidgeting and gesticulating, etc).

He believed the most important facet above was what we look like when we say something. Dr Mehrabian's theory is that what comes out of your mouth doesn't matter if you look as though you have no faith in what you're saying. Consequently, he believed the least important element was the content (ie what we say and the words we use).

There is no doubt that non-verbal communication is important and influential. Putting this in the context of your role as a lawyer and subject-matter expert, however, the content of what you say is much more important than Dr Mehrabian might suggest. As a legal practitioner, the words and the language you use when communicating with others will have a massive impact on the brand you perpetuate. Why? You spend a lot of time on the phone talking to others, you spend a lot of time writing e-mails and letters, and when you're face-to-face in meetings (internally with colleagues or externally with clients) you will be expected to choose your words carefully and deliberately, and to tailor your message to the preferred style of those you need to impress. As such, even if you are a complete master of the non-verbal, if the words you use are poorly considered you will entirely undermine your brand. All style and no substance makes Sebastian a very flashy but pointless boy!

How do you tailor your communication style?

The key lies in preparation and planning. George Bernard Shaw once said, 'I am the most spontaneous speaker in the world, because every word, every gesture, and retort has been carefully rehearsed'. Similarly, the best communicators are those who understand that effective communication is based around a few key rules:

a) Giving the customer (ie the communication recipient) what he wants. How much information does he want to receive from you? How can you prepare for this?

b) Showing the customer the information he wants, ie presenting it in a way the customer understands and which reflects his preferred style.

c) Adapting to what the customer might want, ie being flexible enough to discuss new ideas if raised by the customer when you deliver your information.

In the context of these rules, there are three types of scenarios (or a combination thereof) at work in a law firm where your communication skills will be tested and where you will have the opportunity to make a real, tangible impact on your colleagues:

a) **Formal** — you are delivering a piece of research back to another lawyer, non-lawyer or professional, or you are going into a meeting with a client and *you have time to prepare* (ie you need to impress as a lawyer, as a professional and as a human-being).

b) **Stealth** — you have been ambushed by someone who is demanding answers from you immediately and *you don't have time to prepare* (ie again, you need to impress as a lawyer, as a professional and as a human-being).

c) **Informal** — you are chatting with someone informally and *you don't need to prepare* (ie you are just chatting as a human and not necessarily as a lawyer).

We are not going to spend any time on scenario (c) in this chapter. Why? Because we can assume that you are social creatures, able to hold relaxed conversations and talk about non-work things without planning them too far ahead. After all, you have got this far. You can probably strike up a conversation over a sandwich in the canteen, or over a pint of IPA or glass of Pinot Grigio in the local JD Wetherspoon without overthinking too much.

It is in scenarios (a) and (b) where you can really stand out – but only if you prepare correctly and appropriately. For all three scenarios, however, you should be aware of the importance of holding or carrying yourself well to maximise your positive brand. What does this mean? It means thinking about the following before key communications:

- What do you look like when you speak?
- How do you sound?
- How do you walk?
- How do you introduce yourself?
- How do you stand?
- Do you really listen?
- How enthusiastic do you look?

Let's look at this stuff quickly before moving on to how you might prepare for key communications.

A sense of calm …

Everyone knows that smiling is a good thing. Happy people smile. Open people smile. Charming people smile. Above all, confident, assured people smile. A smile says a lot about a person–friendly, approachable, kind. And we notice immediately when people fail to smile — we often label people as 'miserable so-and-so's' if they are too serious. Smiling is, after all, a basic human emotional manifestation.

The problem is, lawyers tend not to smile that much. Why? Because many lawyers think that to be taken seriously by others, they have to act seriously. This assumption is fundamentally flawed. Serious people are not always serious. Serious people are confident. Confident people are relaxed. Relaxed people are prepared. And most importantly, **prepared** people smile.

Granted, it is much easier to smile in a social context — at a party, meeting new people or with friends in a nice restaurant, with a delicious prawn cocktail starter on its way. After all, what's really to smile about at 16:00 on a rainy, grey, miserable Monday afternoon when you've been asked to type up a note of a conference call that lasted seven hours by 17:30? The answer is probably nothing. But the responsibility is still on you to communicate positively to those around you in everything you do — look happy! Happy doesn't mean loud and 'in your face', it means quiet contentment, understated confidence and the ability always to appear calm when everyone else has gone crackers.

Carrying yourself positively – high status versus low status …

In the theatre world, characters are divided into those that are **high status** and those that are **low status**. As an actor, appreciating the status of your character is a way of understanding how that character might interact with the world around him, so that you are able to alter and tailor your performance accordingly. In other words, a powerful king and a lowly serf would traditionally inhabit opposite status 'spaces'. They would look different and carry themselves differently. If someone playing a powerful king acted in a low status way, like a serf, his character might not be believable. The play might suffer as a result, because the audience might leave the theatre after the show with the impression that the acting was not 'credible'.

Why is this useful for you? Communication is all about status and letting people know what status 'space' you inhabit. Great communicators are high status – not pompous or cocky, just high status. Politics aside, Obama, Blair and Clinton are all great communicators. Yes, they are all highly intelligent, but that's not their defining selling point. They all ooze high status. Odds on that if Obama was a partner of a law firm, he wouldn't need to shout or be aggressive to get things done. You wouldn't feel bossed about by him. You would feel like you were working as a team, inspired and energised. Why? Because high status does not mean dictatorial or bossy. It means assertive and articulate.

'Sure, senior people in law firms can afford to be high-status,' you might be thinking. What about you? Starting out in a hierarchical environment, not sure what you're doing, you don't want to come across as an over-confident upstart or as a meek little mouse. It is a tricky situation and calls for a fine balance; being all high-status assertive without 'boiling over' into arrogance.

Some practical ideas to get the right balance are set out in Table 4.1 below.

Table 4.1 *Balancing your status*

LOW STATUS JUNIOR LAWYER	HIGH STATUS JUNIOR LAWYER
Hovers around doors whilst urgently waiting to speak to a senior colleague who is on the phone, wasting time and irritating others	Sends an e-mail to a busy colleague asking her to let him know when she is free, or asks that person's secretary to call him once the colleague is available

LOW STATUS JUNIOR LAWYER	HIGH STATUS JUNIOR LAWYER
Too risk averse — when given work, [always looks for problems]and sets obstacles before understanding the work properly – presents problems or issues without solutions	Positivity — always smiles and says thanks when receiving work, asking the right questions to ensure she knows exactly what the work entails — always has an idea for a solution to a potential problem or issue and has thought-through, carefully considered ideas ready when they are asked for (and sometimes when they are not!)
Context —does a piece of work in a vacuum without asking for context — what is the bigger picture?	Context — always asks for background when given work to maximise the opportunity for deeper involvement in a matter later down the line. Stays in touch with key people to remain in the frame for further involvement
Arrangement — mis-management — always happy to cancel longstanding arrangements when asked to do urgent work	Arrangement — management — gives notice where possible, is assertive but flexible about important arrangements. Is not the person who always misses her best-friend's 30th birthday
Weak — delegates work apologetically and then disappears, because he is embarrassed	Powerful —delegates work clearly and assertively, and remains available for support

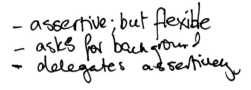

- assertive; but flexible
- asks for background
- delegates assertively

Questions — is afraid of asking questions when faced with aggressive people	Questions— uses a good mixture of <u>open and closed questions</u> when receiving instructions, summarises and stops delegator to check understanding when necessary
Time slave — always flapping and never has enough time — never questions deadlines or asks for real deadline, and never turns up to meetings on time, always cancelling meetings at the last minute	Time manager — <u>manages her diary</u> so that she is always on time and never rushes frantically into or out of meetings **British Army mantra:** if you are five minutes early you're on time, if you're on time you're late
Language— Imposter Syndrome — always self-deprecating in conversation, *'What do I know?!'*	Language — talks confidently about what she knows and admits when she doesn't know
Rapport — always moves straight to business without considering the need for building rapport	Rapport — makes time for some appropriate 'small talk' before moving into the nitty-gritty ...

You shouldn't become pre-occupied with how you might smile, how you might look when you walk, what you should do with your hands and how you should carry yourself when you walk into a room (see Table 4.2 below for some more cosmetic, practical communication skills tips). It's more important that you <u>act with empa</u>thy in applying your communication skills to any given situation. You need to find out and understand what your recipient wants and to meet those expectations (or at least make that person believe you have done so). This should be combined with a few basic rules you should follow to avoid risk and ensure you are not to blame if things go wrong.

Looking the part ...

Table 4.2 Some quick law firm communication skills tips

Handshake and kiss	The webbing (between thumb and index finger) of your hand meets the webbing on the other person's hand, fingers right round the hand and should last for roughly two seconds or two shakes — no longer. There should be no difference in firmness for men or women; as a guide, your handshake should be such that women do not feel discomfort or pain and men do not feel like they are shaking a soggy herring. Never cheek-kiss in England at work. Be aware that this convention might be different when you go abroad. Follow your senior colleagues' lead.
Tea/Coffee	Excluding external client meetings (where the partner in charge often takes responsibility for this), always try to offer tea, coffee or water to your colleagues when starting a meeting with them. Subliminally, it sends a very powerful message of control, confidence, hospitality and assertiveness.
Smile	Smiling when you start a conversation relaxes you and others around you. Be aware that smiling when angry or cross (passive-aggression) is a sure-fire way to undermine others' confidence in you. Smile only when you are genuinely feeling content, confident and/or happy. Although if you're not happy, don't look miserable — it's a complete turn-off.

Listening	You should be listening actively all the time at work. That means direct eye-to-eye contact, leaning in where possible, repeating and summarising regularly and appropriately, and not looking over peoples' shoulders when they talk to you. The recipient of your communication should feel as though he/she is the only person in the world you want to be communicating with at that moment. You should be taking visible notes as you talk and listen, controlling the speed of the conversation to record your thoughts accurately ('Do you mind if we pause for a minute whilst I get that down?')
Walking	Invariably, walking as though you have a purpose is a good thing. Aimlessly wandering around departments or firms is viewed suspiciously by those with the power. Always try to carry a notepad and pen or a document with you, so that you look as if you're on your way to something vaguely important, even if it's the canteen ...
Talking	Powerful people take their time when they talk. So you should talk slowly (or at least slightly more slowly than might feel comfortable to you) and check your recipients' understanding appropriately, especially at the end of complicated points. As a general point, when communicating internally, and time permitting, try to see people face-to-face as much as possible. E-mail is the least effective communication method internally. Your influencing skills are at their most powerful when speaking with someone in person.

Eating	Try not to eat in front of anyone at work unless it is appropriate (eg proper meals!). Eating doesn't look professional. Eat when you have a break, away from your desk and away from those colleagues you might need to impress. If you must snack at your desk, keep it to cold food stuffs that don't make a noise or mess. Crunch and slop is to be avoided, breakfast cereal especially ... Never leave dirty crockery in your office.
Eyes and extras ...	Narrowing your eyes sends a message of distrust to others. So does scratching your neck and fidgeting whilst you speak. Stillness is best, so that your recipient can focus solely on your face and the words coming out of your mouth

SOME LAW FIRM COMMUNICATORS

The practical focus here is on building **internal** relationships and communicating with your **internal** clients, as well as with colleagues you want on-side. However, much of the material we cover below is equally transferable externally. In any event, early on in your career, building trust internally is likely to be the key to maximising your opportunities to build external client relationships. If you can't communicate internally, your supervisor won't unleash you on external (fee-paying) clients!

There are many great models that aim to categorise human beings (at and outside work) according to the way in which they interact with others. You might have come across **Myers Briggs Type Indicator** (MBTI — www.myersbriggs.org), **Belbin Team Roles** theory (www.belbin.com) or the **Social Styles** influence and impact theory (www.tracomcorp.com), and others. All these models involve an element of psychometric testing to find out your preference for a certain style of interaction. You are then in a position to work with your profile to determine how you might amend your style to get the best out of others. These tools are all designed to increase your self-awareness at work.

The problem is that when you are starting out as a junior commercial lawyer (either as a new or seat-changing trainee, or as an NQ/junior lawyer), you will be in a brand new team and a brand new environment. You will be flying by the seat of your pants, you will have very little professional self-awareness but you will still need to communicate effectively from day one to stand out and create a positive brand. You most probably won't have time to sit down and do psychometric tests, to intraspect or to delve into your own social preferences according to a theoretical model. You just need to impress those for whom you work by communicating effectively — simple!

And you won't find it difficult to communicate with certain types of people in your firm —the straightforward, nice, amenable, rational, calm and generous ones. They are relatively easy to impress if you don't act like an idiot but think commercially. Your real challenge lies in meeting the communication expectations of the demanding, difficult, ego-driven, contradictory and potentially undermining people you might come across in any work place — but especially in commercial law firms.

The Social Styles theory, mentioned above, separates people into four types (Analytical, Driver, Expressive and Amiable). It is worth visiting this theory (and even trying to find out your profile) at work to supplement your own self-awareness. Building on the Social Styles theory in a legal context, however, the biggest communication challenge you will face as a junior lawyer in a commercial firm is in preparing and planning for interactions with three types of business people, specifically:

- The Rhino Communicator

- The Scientist Communicator

- The Schmoozer Communicator

We will look at how you might communicate with each type below. It is worth noting, however, that these are only models and caricatures. The rules set out for each 'type' will not work across the board. You will rarely find one type in its purest form. More likely is that you will come across lawyers and non-lawyers with a preference for one of the three styles but an outward-facing persona that bridges all of them. And you too will find your own preference over time. Until then, it is important that you are aware of the symptoms and characteristics of all three, to help increase your ability to straddle them all, to appraise your own style and to be more self-aware when you communicate.

When you start out, you will simply have to adapt. Like a chameleon, you will have to change your communication style to reflect that of your recipient from minute to minute. And that will not be easy. Sometimes you will be communicating with an individual you have not come across before. You won't know what preference they have. In these situations, you will have to tool yourself up; asking others (another junior lawyer, trainee or secretary) what they are like to work with. You can then apply some of the rules below to maximise your impact.

Let's take a look.

The Rhino

Psychology

Rhinos tend to be quite senior and successful. For Rhinos, it is about power and results. It is about the destination and not the journey. In GCSE mathematics-terms, with the Rhino you don't get any marks for the workings-out if your answer is wrong. Whilst they might be charming when they need to be, Rhinos don't feel the need to be liked and they certainly don't need to like you. They are mistakes focused, and any bridge you build with them is likely to topple over quickly and terminally if things go wrong. Often, they have no time for people they see as weak or meek. This is not because they are necessarily nasty people, they are just ruthlessly efficient and pragmatic. They don't have the time. They do, however, respond well to a bit of appropriate push-back.

Characteristics

Rhinos don't have time to chat; they won't be outwardly interested in what you did at the weekend and have no interest in telling you what their favourite hobby is. Private lives are private and work is for work. Rapport does not tend to be a big part of their equation. Light-hearted chat is not desirable and body language is deliberate. This is not because Rhinos are intrinsically rude but because it takes too much time to make chit-chat. As such, interactions can be quite rushed and/or intense. Rhinos might bark instructions out, and they will often try to fit a 20-minute internal meeting into a 10-minute slot because they have double-booked with something more important. Or worse, they won't turn up to a meeting at all. This is not because they are careless or intentionally rude, but because they aspire towards uber-efficiency and not spending too long on any one matter or issue. They are solutions — and not detail-focused, will go with their 'gut', and don't have a lot of time for background information and discussion. They will notice, however, if you make a mistake, and it is likely that they will be reluctant to work with you again. They have no time for regular constructive criticism or feedback. They work long hours, and they might shout and scream when they are stressed (and even when they are relaxed!); they don't appear to care about being socially unpopular. They have a high level of self-confidence.

Recognising a Rhino – at school...

Rhinos were either terrible bullies or terribly bullied at school. If it was the latter, they are now getting their own back ... If it was the former, they are simply carrying on the 'good' work.

Recognising a Rhino – at work...

They might wear trendy, expensive clothes that don't necessarily suit them. They might be out of shape, as they spend too much time at work or in the pub charming clients. They might drive cars and SUVs that they don't need or suit, and they might well be single into their late 30s because they haven't made time for relationships. Their offices might be decorated in a rather Spartan way (deal trophies galore if they are transactional solicitors ...). They rarely turn up for anything that isn't chargeable. Because they are so results-focused, they are often very successful. They might not smile a lot and words are not wasted when they talk.

Some general rules for communicating with Rhinos

- If meeting a Rhino for the first time, establish credibility early on with a firm handshake, a confident smile and your title (trainee, NQ or associate) and background (briefly!).

- Whatever you do, be on time for all meetings with Rhinos.

- Be prepared to move straight to legal-technical/commercial discussion.

- Don't bother asking how they are or, worse, how their weekend was unless they mention it first.

- If they are stressed, you should be prepared to display a similar sense of urgency, not necessarily behaving like a Rhino (shouting, screaming, etc) but at least showing you are planning to move fast, act urgently and treat this with the appropriate sense of 'now'.

- Have provisional solutions and a plan of action ready for the Rhino to review (especially around external client-care or pricing matters).

- Reassure the Rhino that you are on top of the legal-technical detail.

- Always have an agenda for meetings, with clear actions points and follow-up (most of which you will be responsible for).

- Be prepared to ask Rhinos to repeat instructions, especially complex, delegated legal-technical work, when they rush through a meeting – they respond well to assertiveness, but will take advantage if you are meek.

- Always ask how they want to receive the work (format and delivery — by hand, by e-mail or by phone?).

- Always ask Rhinos if they want you to work in a particular way. For example, do they have a starting point for the work in mind? Is there anything you should not cover or include when doing work for them?

- Offer potential solutions and explain which course you intend to follow quickly (and without much detail).

- After your meeting with Rhinos, don't feel the need to update them with your progress as you go along. Just get them the answer or completed memo by the agreed deadline. If they ask for an update, respond quickly and efficiently.

- Be smartly dressed when communicating with a Rhino. Presume a high level of formality to ensure you don't come across to them as unprofessional.

- Be prepared to discuss money with Rhinos. Figures, billing and fees are extremely important to them. Although they don't want the detail, have all facts and figures prepared in case they ask for them.

- Rhinos prefer quick, face-to-face meetings, and will not reliably respond to e-mail and written communications. You cannot assume a Rhino has read an e-mail just because he might have received it. In fact, Rhinos will often deny having seen any e-mails you sent to them. If this happens, put a quick meeting in their diary (through their secretary), and go and see them with a summary print-out of correspondence and documentation (relevant sections highlighted). Re-sending e-mails with a 'I look forward to hearing from you ...' or 'If I don't hear from you I will assume ...' at the end will not work.

The Scientist

Psychology

You can assume that all successful lawyers have an element of this type about them. It's all about the minutiae. The Scientist revels in detail. It doesn't matter how long it takes as long as it is correct. That means 100 per cent correct. Mistakes (especially of the grammatical variety) offend the Scientist. Just like a complex scientific equation, everything has to be precise and all due diligence has to be completed before a task is undertaken. No decisions are made until all avenues have been explored. All resources must be utilised and time accounted for with long narratives in the time-recording software. Scientists will worry if left to their own devices and if kept 'out of the loop'. Scientists find it hard to switch off and relax. They will often work very long hours as a symptom of their neurotic, detail-driven obsession. Scientists are highly intellectual, but they are often practically inefficient.

Characteristics

Scientists love structure and (exploring) options. They are often quiet people who don't respond particularly well to excitable enthusiasm, preferring cautious optimism based on facts and figures, rather than 'gut' feelings and grand, strategic plans. They won't make a decision quickly without covering all exits, and will expect you to display a clear enthusiasm for the legal-technical detail. They won't tell you much about their private lives unless you really take time to build rapport and trust.

Recognising a Scientist − at school...

Scientists were not cool at school. However, they probably weren't un-cool. Most just kept their heads down at school and worked hard. They got straight As all the way through, and have been academically brilliant since leaving school.

Recognising a Scientist − at work...

They might wear conservative clothing (grey suits and ties, trouser-suits for women), drive conservative cars (a Volvo, FIAT, Ford or Peugeot) and have very stable relationships (invariably with another lawyer). They might tell you they hate 'public speaking' and prefer e-mailing to large meetings. They will probably love routine, have the same lunch most days and rarely get angry or show extremes of emotion, often keeping religiously fit (Scientists are often in good or reasonable physical shape). Scientists are often excellent legal practitioners.

Some general rules for dealing with Scientists

- Internal team or workgroup meetings with a Scientist will take longer than you imagine — book more time than you think you need and keep them in the loop with the arrangements before the meeting. Before sending out calendar invites, ask them if there is anyone else they would like to invite.

- Be sure to send them an agenda for the meeting before it takes place, and give them time to add their points. You need to ensure all meetings have clear actions. Be prepared for more meetings, follow-up meetings and meetings to discuss meetings!

- Make sure you have all relevant information for them to examine. Scientists will want to see background material, case law, pricing information, facts and figures. Unsubstantiated statements will be meaningless to a Scientist without explanatory information.

- Meetings with Scientists have to be managed carefully to ensure they don't get lost in the detail. You need to reassure them constantly that things are being done so they don't worry when you leave the room.

- Don't rush a Scientist, never shout or display obvious extremes of emotion.

- Don't feel the need to build a rapport with a Scientist. Rapport is replaced with detail for them. They build trust with others by immersing themselves in such detail. Like the Rhino, their private lives are mostly private.

- Scientists like certainty of communication. When discussing anything with them, using phrases like 'I reckon ...', and 'I think ...' or 'My gut feeling is ...' will antagonise them if made in a vacuum.

- Don't poke fun at Scientists. They rarely laugh at themselves and don't enjoy jokes for the sake of jokes. If they make a joke, however, laugh as if it's genuinely funny – then move on quickly to more detail without dwelling on it. Feel free to poke fun at yourself. This will help the Scientist relax in your company.

- Don't offer solutions before a Scientist has had the opportunity to explore all the options. Ask Scientists to give their opinions first, and then contribute your thoughts based around their input, after asking permission to contribute: *'Do you mind if I offer my thoughts?'* In the meeting, ask them how they would like you to keep them informed as you go along.

- Ask them for their feedback regularly so they feel as though they retain an element of control. Always act upon feedback and show you are doing so.

- Scientists prefer a mixture of face-to-face and written communication. Always follow-up a meeting with an e-mail, and follow-up the e-mail with another e-mail to check progress. Never assume Scientists are happy; always check.

The Schmoozer

Psychology

Schmoozers are primarily concerned with building relationships whilst at the same time massaging their own egos. A Schmoozer might be socially insecure, wanting to be liked by all. However, Schmoozers also want to be respected. They might be softer human beings than Rhinos, but they are just as ambitious, preferring milder methods to get things done. They enjoy establishing rapport and will appear to be quite ideas-driven, sometimes skirting over the finer detail to get to the exciting stuff quickly. They might lose enthusiasm quickly.

Characteristics

In communication terms, Schmoozers are all about chatting. They will happily chat about their weekends and their hobbies. They will ask you about yours (not necessarily listening), but something will pop into their heads mid-conversation that might impede their ability to maintain a two-way conversation. They tend to be on 'transmit' more than 'receive', and don't respond well to cold, hard business talk 100 per cent of the time. They smile a lot and enjoy informality.

Recognising a Schmoozer – at school...

Schmoozers were clever, popular and extroverted. They might have fallen into law because they weren't sure what else to do, having done a degree in English Literature, History or Politics, or Human Geography (BA). They tended to be sporty, amusing and a lot of fun.

Recognising a Schmoozer – at work...

Schmoozers dress well, aren't overtly money-obsessed, despite being well off, and seem to be content. If senior, they have a very loyal client base and spend a lot of time engaging in business-development activities. They have lunch in the canteen, and have many friends across the firm and a high profile cross-departmentally. Many of their meetings will be held in the coffee shop or an equally informal environment. They tend to do a lot of presenting and get involved in the delivery of internal and external training, enjoying the 'soft' skills side of their jobs. They might regularly muck in with Learning & Development or Graduate Recruitment initiatives. They do, however, spend most of the time talking about themselves, their family and their achievements, and it is a little tiring to hold a long conversation with them. They laugh at a lot when they talk, and seem to enjoy life (even if, underneath, they might be miserable).

Some general rules for dealing with Schmoozers

- Don't make the mistake of moving straight to business with Schmoozers. They will appear to want to take time to get to know you and find out about non-work issues that might affect you.

- As such, when meeting with a Schmoozer, make sure you budget for a bit of time at the start (before moving to business) and at the end of the meeting (before rushing off) to discuss non-work matters.

- Asking Schmoozers open questions about themselves builds trust with them; it massages their egos. With that in mind, take your lead from them as to how much you might give away about yourself.

- Schmoozers will more openly discuss feelings than Rhinos or Scientists, so don't be afraid of telling them if you feel nervous or unhappy about something. However, make sure you don't push all the responsibility on to them to find solutions. They might also worry.

- Schmoozers will waste a lot of time in conversation at work discussing peripheral issues (eg grand ideas for marketing or business development initiatives), so you will have to re-focus their energies if time is of the essence (eg agendas in meetings are a must!).

- Active listening is a must for Schmoozers; they want to feel you are interested in them as 'people' and not just as 'colleagues'. Make sure you show you have listened by asking them related and linked questions once they have spoken.

- Schmoozers thrive on face-to-face interaction and engagement. As such, they prefer not to do things via e-mail. If you e-mail them, make sure you follow-up in person and ask for their input and ideas (even if you don't use them). Always follow up with a phone call. Schmoozers will not read a long e-mail chain if they are cc'd. Follow up with them individually to ensure they understand what it is you need from them.

MAXIMISING YOUR COMMUNICATING IMPACT ACROSS THE BOARD

When you are senior, powerful, successful and rich, you can communicate in any way you choose. However, those who are most successful when they start out in commercial firms do well because they are able to find the 'middle ground' in communication-style terms. They are not Rhinos, Scientists or Schmoozers in any obvious way. Although they might have a preference for one particular style, they are able to widen their appeal by finding the lowest common denominator across all three styles, acting it out in a very broadly accessible way and pleasing everyone, moving in and out of the appropriate style when it becomes necessary. Once they are more experienced, they can focus more on following the rules specific to each individual style and carving their own communication style 'niche'.

However, they have to earn that right. In the meantime, to achieve a broad preferential appeal, you might want to adhere to the 'cross-communication style' rules set out in Table 4.3 below when communicating with any fellow lawyers or non-lawyers (you might need or want to impress) at work.

Table 4.3 Cross-communication style rules

Stage	Actions
At the outset of the relationship	• Find out from others who have worked with them what their style might be and any communication 'quirks' they might have. • If the above doesn't work, ask your recipient how he/she wants to be communicated with and stick to it. A simple 'how would you like me to let you know/keep you in the loop?' should do the trick. Don't over-think it!
Before your interactions (ie phone and face-to-face)	• Budget for 15 per cent extra time that might be taken up with chit-chat. • Always have an agenda and be very deliberate and clear in your arrangements for meetings. • Send your agenda at least 3 hours before the meeting or phone call. • Always put a blurb in a meeting request explaining what the meeting is for. • Always assume meetings will run over and do not arrange to be somewhere else immediately after the meeting or phone call. • Have all the facts and figures at your disposal. Think of all the questions your recipient might ask and have answers ready. This includes having copies of all relevant documents (enough for you and everyone else at the meeting or on the phone). • Consider using visual aids (eg handout or flipchart) to help your recipient understand and assimilate the information.

Stage	Actions
	• Find out what your recipient is hoping to achieve from the meeting — ask him/her or someone in his/her team.
	• Don't go with 'gut feelings' or use phrases like '*I believe*', '*I think*' or '*I reckon*'. Instead use deliberate, clear, categorical language.
	• Be ready to present ideas for provisional solutions to any problems should they demand ideas from you.
	• Check the arrangements for the meeting. Is the room big enough? Are there enough seats? Has lunch been ordered?
During your interactions	• Always arrive to a meeting 5 minutes early and call someone on the phone on time to the minute!
	• In rapport-building terms, always follow the lead of your recipient — a neat 'How are you?' is a good 'in', but don't go further unless he/she gives you a detailed answer, and then reciprocate.
	• Explain how long you will keep your recipient — don't underestimate!
	• A firm handshake is a must if you are meeting someone for the first time — remember, it is two firm shakes and then release. Good eye contact should be maintained, with an open smile during the handshake. Any more than two shakes and it becomes creepy and an invasion of personal space; any fewer and it is pointless.
	• At the outset always explain the objectives of the meeting (what to cover) if organised by you. Also be prepared to explain the desired outcomes (what the attendees will take away) if someone asks.

	• Stay away from extremes of emotion during interactions.
	• Talk about non-work issues and matters only if asked directly by your recipient.
	• Start with open questions, moving to closed questions quickly if the circumstances so dictate.
	• Use reassuring language like '*I will take care of that*' and '*Leave that with me, I'll come back to you by ...*' wherever possible.
	• At the end, summarise action points and take responsibility for as many as you can manage. Ask how they would like to receive updates on these points.
	• If you haven't covered everything you need to cover, suggest a follow-up and be clear as to when that might take place.
After your interactions	• Always follow-up with an e-mail, summarising action points and organising any extra meetings required, within 24 hours.
	• Make sure to follow up on any specific action points for which you were responsible, with appropriate progress reports.
	• Stay in touch — send your recipient an e-mail in a couple of days to check that he/she is happy with the results of your interaction, and whether anything else has surfaced he/she would like you to deal with.

Add to this … learning styles

To maximise your impact when communicating, it is also worth noting that people tend to have different preferences for taking on information or learning. Without delving too deeply into the technical theory, people tend to fall into three categories:

a) **Visual**, ie they remember more if they see things (eg the people who can sit through a two-hour PowerPoint presentation without falling asleep).

b) **Auditory**, ie they remember more if they hear things (eg the people who can listen to a podcast on 'Pure Economic Loss' for 90 minutes without killing themselves).

c) **Kinaesthetic**, ie they remember more if they do and experience things (eg the people who like to write stuff down or 'have a go' as they listen).

What does this mean for you? It means that on top of the communication rules set out above, you need to think about how you **transfer** information to your recipient (not just **how** you **communicate** it). To maximise your impact when you don't know the learning preference of your recipient, you should always ask yourself the following questions before walking into a room or delivering information:

- *Can I give them something to look at whilst I talk (visual preference), eg handout, print-out, copy-document, (especially important if you are on the phone)?*

- *Am I leaving space for them to ask questions, or am I just talking at them non-stop?*

- *Can I show them what I am talking about to involve them by drawing it on a white-board or flipchart?*

- *Do they need context (eg example or extract documents) to add a kinaesthetic element to the experience?*

It's for you...

Making an impact on the phone (where the majority of your external 'meetings' will take place) is vital as a junior commercial lawyer. This means acting professionally, confidently and in a careful, proactive and structured way.

How might you achieve this? Table 4.4 below gives some tips.

Table 4.4 *Communicating externally on the phone — some helpful hints*

With an external client (also relevant for external experts)	Where possible, send an e-mail beforehand explaining the purpose, date, time and estimated duration of call.
	Reiterate timings at the start of the call.
	Ask clients if they have anything they would like to add to the agenda before the call.
	Send an agenda through for them to print out and annotate as you sequence through the items.
	Smile when you start the call — smiling helps moderate your tone of voice and softens your approach.
	Keep your clients apprised of the time as you go through the call.
	Check understanding regularly, particularly after complicated discussion points.
	Summarise at the end of the call, and follow up within two hours with an e-mail which sets out actions and follow-up points (including marked-up agenda).

With the other side	Circulate a draft agenda with your firm's name on it — this shows you are in charge of the structure for the meeting.
	Ask the other side if they have anything they would like to add to the agenda before the call.
	Reiterate the purpose of the call when it begins.
	Smile when you start the call — smiling helps moderate your tone of voice and softens your approach.
	Check understanding regularly, particularly after complicated discussion points, making sure responsibilities are recorded.
	Summarise responsibilities at the end of the call, and follow-up within two hours with an e-mail which sets out actions and follow-up points (including marked-up agenda).

It is always more effective to meet face-to-face with colleagues or clients. Every time you plan a phone call, therefore, consider whether it might be more appropriate to maximise your impact by going round to see them, especially if the news or information you are delivering is bad, important or very good.

If a phone call is the only way, there is a tool to help you to structure those conversations early on in your career when you might have little or no experience of professional phone etiquette. Create your own document around the template set out on the page opposite, consider printing off a few copies and keeping a pile of them next to your phone. Complete one before you dial your recipients' number for the first couple of weeks or months (or until you feel confident in your own structure style). Bonus points will be available here from those who see you completing this form in such a careful, organised manner!

Communicating by Telephone

PREPARATORY SHEET

DATE:

TIME OF CALL (from when to when …):

YOU ARE CALLING (name & position):

THEIR TELEPHONE NUMBER IS:

MATTER THIS RELATES TO (including matter number):

WHAT DO YOU WANT TO DISCUSS?

WHAT DO THEY WANT TO DISCUSS?

WHAT DO YOU NEED THEM TO DO (ACTIONS)?

WHO DO YOU NEED TO DISCUSS THIS WITH?

ACTIONS:

ANY PROBLEMS & ANY PROVISIONAL SOLUTIONS:

POINTS TO INCLUDE IN A VOICEMAIL MESSAGE (never speak for more than 15 seconds on a voicemail function):

AOB (eg house-keeping and follow-up):

Telephone ambush!

Sometimes you will receive an urgent call out of the blue. You might not be able to plan a strategy for dealing with that person, but the onus will still be on you to manage the call assertively. Sometimes you might be able to postpone the call until you have had time to consider the issues. Often, however, your caller will have picked up the phone in a blind panic (clients — internal and external — tend to do this a lot, you will find). You need to deal with this effectively and efficiently right there and then, without automatically deflecting your caller with a *'Can I come back to you?'*. (If you constantly deflect, your clients will wonder why they are paying your fees (external) or giving you work (external and internal).)

So, how do you manage this? The answer is to ask the right questions. People who are panicky and stressed want to be listened to (it is cathartic), and then managed and reassured. They don't want to be immediately palmed off and/or deflected. Asking them open questions (ie questions that don't require a simple yes/no answer), and then listening carefully and deliberately before reacting appropriately, is an excellent way of defusing tension.

Open questions and communications that begin to manage panicky incoming phone calls are:

- What has **happened**?

- Can you **tell me how I can help**?

- What would you **like me to do** for you?

- Can you **take me through** what happened?

- I **understand** why you are worried/upset. I'll take care of this for you, is there anything you would like me to do first?

- I will **come back to you** by ... with ...

- **Don't worry** about this, I'll take care of it.

- Can I just **check you are happy** with what I am planning to do?

- **[Only after you have established the background]** I would like to discuss this with XXX/one of my colleagues who has specific experience in this area before I give you a definitive answer. **Can you tell me when you are free today for me to come back to you?**

Once you have been given more information, you should take control of the phone call using the rules we have already examined above. If you still need time to consider the issues, be clear on deadlines, come up with a mini-project plan and communicate this to your recipient, seeking their approval at each stage. Make sure you give yourself enough time to get your bits and bobs done!

A PRACTICAL APPLICATION OF SOME OF THE COMMUNICATION RULES

So far we have looked at:

a) the elements of effective communication; and

b) how you might spot and deal with different communicators at work.

It is also worth considering two specific communication situations that often occur when you are junior:

a) receiving work from/working with quite a difficult Rhino you nevertheless need to impress; and

b) receiving work from/working with someone who is in a rush and has no time for building rapport.

On the basis of what we have covered so far, it might be worth considering these two real-work scenarios in the following way:

Scenario — *providing context in terms of the larger issues at the heart of any given situation at work*

Issues — *associated with that scenario*

Solutions — *practical steps to take in dealing with your issues*

SCENARIO 1: a difficult Rhino delegator ...

SCENARIO: You have been called into an aggressive Rhino's office to receive some work. You have heard on the grapevine that this Rhino doesn't trust 'juniors' and is unpleasant to deal with. However, the Rhino works with cracking clients and tends to delegate good work with a high level of responsibility.

ISSUES: Making the right impact, getting to the point and showing you mean business quickly, delivering what the Rhino wants, pre-empting problems and stumbling blocks, and following up effectively.

SOLUTIONS:

- Be as smartly dressed as possible, offer a strong hand-shake (standing up with good eye contact and a smile) if you haven't met before and a short introduction explaining who you are (no longer than 10 seconds).

- Have with you copies of all relevant documentation, and hand copies to him/her at the start if you intend to refer to them at any point.

- Deliberately open your notepad in view and put a title at the top of the relevant page (meeting title, meeting with, time and date of meeting), being careful to tilt your notepad so that your recipient can see your notes as you take them.

- Active listening throughout; open questions leading to closed questions to confirm detail – don't speak too much!

- Don't react to any personal attack or rudeness; smile and ignore ...

- Confirm instructions at the end of the brief and state your next steps.

- Thank and close the meeting, asking how the recipient would like to be kept in the loop (eg *'How would you like to receive progress updates?'*).

- Confirm actions from the meeting by e-mail when back at your desk, summarising issues, particularising actions and taking responsibility for as many points as possible.

- Meet expectations regarding deadlines to the minute.

SCENARIO 2: a rushed delegator ...

SCENARIO: Someone has just popped into your office on their way to a meeting to give you some work that needs to be completed within a tight time-frame. You are in the middle of something else that requires a high level of concentration when they start instructing you without warning.

ISSUES: Assertiveness in breaking from your immediate task to listen to the delegator, getting the right instructions, eliminating the risk of poor instructions and the wasting of your time, managing the conversation so that instructions are delivered at an appropriate speed.

SOLUTIONS:
- Apologise and explain that you need to pause from your current work/ job; take a few seconds to manage this carefully and deliberately; apologise for keeping the delegator waiting.

- Take out a separate notepad and pen, deliberately moving your chair away from your computer screen to show engagement, following the same rules for taking notes as in the previous scenario, smiling and leaning in to listen actively.

- Make sure you stop the delegator if he/she starts rushing the instructions, explaining that you want to ensure you get them right before the delegator disappears into his/her meeting; quickly repeat back all key points (both simple and complex).

- Regularly repeat back actions and discrete tasks as they are delegated, so that you are both clear what you will be doing.

- Establish an initial action plan and ask if there is anywhere the delegator would prefer you to start.

- Always establish the next steps and the next point of face-to-face contact to show you are interested in building that trusted relationship.

- Again, follow up by e-mail within 10 minutes of the briefing, explaining your plan of action and strategy. The delegator will see the message popping into his/her e-mail account on his/her Blackberry — most impressive!

SUMMARY – TOP COMMUNICATION TIPS

- Positivity is the key — always smile and walk with purpose wherever you go. Think high status!

- Listen deliberately and actively, summarising regularly and assertively if you lose the thread.

- Ask those around you what your senior colleagues are like, and tailor your communication style appropriately.

- Always have an agenda for every meeting you arrange.

- Never outwardly panic, especially on the phone.

- Make good eye contact when you talk.

- Keep your head and body still when you talk, as a general rule.

- Use open questions to stifle aggression and extremes of emotion in others before making suggestions.

5

Be Client-Focused – Commerciality is not Rocket Science

'Do you have a good grasp of commercial awareness?'
'Are you thinking commercially?'
'I think we need to understand their commercial goals'
'Let's be commercial about this ...'

These rather hackneyed phrases are a firm favourite with lawyers in commercial practice. Although they are over-used in both conversation and correspondence, they are also over-used in appraisal processes, both formally and informally. This means understanding the expectations placed on you in this regard will be vital to your success as a junior lawyer.

Getting to grips with 'commerciality' and 'commercial awareness' will terrify you when you begin your career. You will not know what 'commerciality' is, how to show it, or indeed how to acquire it. You might panic. You might even sweat a little. But fear not: commerciality is nothing to be afraid of when you are starting out. In fact, ironically, it gets harder the more senior you become. What, then, is it?

WHAT IS COMMERCIALITY?

Differing viewpoints

Some say that commercial awareness is something you acquire after practising or being in business for a significant period of time. Others (likely to be more uptight as human beings) will tell you that commerciality is about having a specific knowledge set — being-up-to-date with the markets, and having an almost intimate understanding of the economic variables that affect the way lawyers and business people act and work.

At this stage in your career, neither of these positions is applicable. We examined styles of communication in the previous chapter, but really commerciality is simply an extension of those skills; a facet of effective communication in a commercial law firm. It involves tweaking your thought processes to communicate and show to those around you that you care about the business in which you find yourself.

What are these tweaks? How should you be acting? What should you do, practically, to show you care and convince those in control that you are worth investing in as a lawyer?

The starting point is to think about what being 'commercial' actually means when you are starting out.

No, wait, I think I just had a commercial thought ...

We have already established that your client group comprises both external (fee-paying) and internal (career-controlling) sets. We have explored the importance of treating everyone you come across in a professional capacity as a client, aiming to provide a uniform quality service to enhance your prospects of success. So, if this is the case, it seems ridiculous to think of commerciality only as knowing about business. This is because, in essence, the rules for commerciality and commercial awareness are the same as those for good communication — giving the customer what he wants. Good commercial behaviour is rooted in good communication.

The two things are inextricably linked — an effective twenty-first-century solicitor will think commercially about everything he/she does, and will communicate or signpost it clearly to those who control his/her success.

A tweaked thought process

When, as a junior lawyer, someone asks you if you have good commercial awareness, appraises you on the basis of your commerciality or asks you to think commercially, that person is posing the following questions:

*Do you **understand** your clients (internal and external), do you **identify** with them, are you helping them achieve **their** objectives and are you showing a **passion** for your chosen career?*

This seems obvious. Remember, however, that becoming a lawyer means you are tacitly consenting to working in a service industry, committing to servicing others' needs and wants, and making every effort to be liked and respected by those people. If you are not interested in thinking about your clients (internal and external) and what they want, why choose law for a career? After all, if you are a commercial or corporate solicitor, you chose to work in business. Not in the arts. Not in healthcare. Not in the media. In business. Pure and simple. So, you should expect those around you to want you to show an interest in their business. After all, no one in your law firm will ask you to do work for fun, or for simple intellectual pleasure.

Think of yourself as a car and of your engine as the study and application of the law. Your steering wheel, pedals and chassis, however, are the business influences that guide and drive your activities. Business decides the direction in which your car goes, what it looks like when it drives and how fast it is. Business also tells you when you need to stop, think and refuel. If you put the wrong fuel into the car, it will break down, irrespective of the quality of the engine parts. And if you drive badly and erratically, your licence will be taken away from you.

Your legal colleagues (especially the senior ones) will, of course, be interested in the law – it's their bread and butter. Because of the demands placed upon them by external clients, however, the successful ones will also be very interested in business and the commercial aspects of the deal, matter or transaction. In other words, what does X piece of law mean in practical, tangible terms? How will it affect the bottom line? How will it affect the long- and short-term strategic aims of that company, or individual or your firm? Commercial lawyers are obliged to think in this way because external clients and non-lawyers are not (on the whole) interested in law. Unless they ask you to shower them with technical know-how, you can assume that they think discussing and debating technical legal issues is boring, slightly irritating and quite pompous. So, being able to identify these commercial elements and aspects is a key skill. Signposting your knowledge and understanding of these elements to others with whom you work (as well as demonstrating the requisite technical competence) is vital if you want to be respected.

Success or failure

Dictionary.com defines 'commercial' as being *'prepared, done, or acting with sole or chief emphasis on saleability, profit, or success'*. The key word is **success**. The law is very effective at presenting problems or hurdles that can stifle business progress and success. Being commercial in your outlook means being **success-** or **solutions-focused**. In other words, commercial people are solutions-driven, positive in outlook and show a keen interest in helping others to achieve success in a business context, whatever that success might look like. How do you find out what that success might look like? You ask them.

Helping others to achieve success in a business context

At your level, being commercial is about using common sense in a business environment, giving the customer what he wants, asking appropriate questions, displaying a passion for success (both personally and for others) and a hunger to be involved. It is no more than that. Sure, there are things you can read to give your business knowledge an 'edge', but really it is about showing an interest in the career you have chosen. The rest you will learn on the job.

THE EXPECTATIONS PLACED UPON YOU

You know you've made it when you know what you know and you know what you don't know and you're prepared to admit it ... (senior equity partner, City of London law firm)

No one will expect you to have a sophisticated, bird's-eye understanding of business or commerce to begin with. They will, however, expect you to recognise where you need to improve or fill in the knowledge gaps, and to show an interest in spotting those gaps.

In other words, junior **commercial** lawyers show their commerciality by:

a) being enthusiastic and willing;

b) asking for context (not just content, in being a tiny jigsaw piece) and feedback (incorporating where appropriate);

c) showing an ability to focus on the objectives rather than just on the legal procedure.

A happy lawyer is a busy lawyer. Being busy means productivity. Getting stuff done feels better than strategising, evaluating and reviewing what might, might not or has been done. Strategising, however, is important. Getting the objectives and outcomes clear before jumping into the next project is one of the key commercial skills for a twenty-first-century solicitor. And this applies most tangibly to you, as a junior apprentice.

It tastes the same but looks and feels different

Why do people think the supermarket chain Waitrose is posh? Why is Waitrose so successful as a supermarket despite the mark-up it places on its goods? Why are people prepared to pay more for something they might be able to get for a third less down the road?

The answer is an inner, subconscious feeling that shoppers are buying and experiencing real quality. Sure, some of that is down to branding and packaging. Waitrose might take a can of bog-standard chick peas, put the words 'Morroccan-style' in front of the word 'Chick', plaster a high resolution picture of a child eating the said chick peas in his sunny kitchen and smiling on the front, add a vivid, modern font theme, put the product in a tidy, smart, modern aisle dedicated to 'North African' foods and charge 50p more. Why? Because the buyer would think the chick peas were of a better quality. Would they taste the same as those bought from the cheaper competitor? Of course. Would the buyer return to Waitrose and buy those chick peas again? Probably. Why? Because shopping in Waitrose leaves shoppers feeling as though they have had a quality experience: from the decor and the packaging, to the staff and the range — it all says top-notch. Many customers won't mind paying a bit more; they feel it is worth it. Even if it isn't, they want to go back.

How is this relevant to commerciality? Great junior lawyers leave everyone they work with feeling as though they too have had a quality experience. They are enthusiastic, loyal, positive, driven, hungry to learn, service-focused, results- and solutions-oriented, pragmatic and realistic about their own limitations, seeking feedback to improve performance wherever they can. Following the Waitrose analogy, others are willing to invest in them despite the fact that it might cost them more in terms of the time they have to spend developing them. This is because they feel it is worthwhile. Like the chick peas in the posh can, you might not be any better as a technical lawyer than your colleague, but the way you package yourself and manage your brand screams success – both for you and for those with whom you work.

I think what you have done is clever but I don't think it's got any legs, so I'm out ...

BBC's 'Dragon's Den' is a great TV format. It is exciting, it is interesting and it is modern. And most of all, it is all about commerciality. And as commercially sophisticated as the entrepreneurs are, they all have to speak in a language that viewers will understand to ensure TV ratings success. It's an interesting balance. Whilst the 'dragons' are looking for great ideas and ideas people, they are also looking for commercial pragmatists who understand the investors' need to get a financial return on their investments.

Watch one episode of this brilliant show and you will hear all kinds of questions that focus on the similar commercial issues (in brackets) you might consider when working as a commercial solicitor:

- *Who are you? (Why should I listen to you?)*
- *Did you even consider the risks before starting out? (Have you planned for every outcome?)*
- *Have you ever asked yourself who your end-user is? (Do you know what your customer really wants?)*
- *Why should I invest? (Show me your passion, give me ideas!)*
- *How am I going to get my money back and how long will it take? (Give me the cold, hard facts and figures, and all the pragmatic options.)*
- *What are your goals for this business? (How will this play out in the short- and long-term?)*
- *Can you show this business has legs? (How can you reassure me that this is the best course of action?)*
- *What do you need my expertise for? (What is the result you need to achieve?)*
- *What would you like me to do for you? (How would you like me to go about this? Do you have any starting point in mind?)*

These clever questions are designed to clarify goals, establish reality and close in on pragmatic objectives as distinct from big ideas and pipe-dreams. After all, why should the entrepreneurs give their hard-earned cash to someone who has no idea how their business might benefit the bottom line? It is not a charity show. Neither is your law firm. Lawyers can be quite uncharitable, negatively judgemental and reluctant to take unnecessary risks. Especially on you, if you aren't on top of your game.

Investing in you?

With all of this in mind, as if preparing to face a panel of senior partners in a 'Dragon's Den' scenario and asking them to invest in your work and career, you should ask yourself the following questions before all key interactions, and intermittently at work:

- *Do I always consider the appropriateness of the format in which I present myself?*

- *Do I always consider who will benefit from the work I undertake?*

- *Do I always consider the needs and goals of my end-user?*

- *Do I show a passion for generating and assisting in the implementation of new ideas and suggestions?*

- *Do I understand the industry/industries of my end-user(s) and/or investors to be able to display the requisite empathy?*

- *Is my idea carefully thought through, with clear objectives and outcomes? Or will senior partner Peter Jones declare himself 'out' before I have finished speaking, for appearing 'wishy-washy'?*

- *Am I trying to be too wacky and ideas-driven?*

- *Do I visibly panic when pushed away from my plan?*

- *Do I always have the cold, hard facts and figures at my disposal should I need them?*

- *Am I enthusiastic, speaking from the heart without extremes of emotion?*

- *Do I express myself confidently and articulately, using the appropriate language?*

- *Do I look the part? Would I embarrass myself or my colleagues if I was taken to a meeting looking the way I do, or dressed the way I am?*

- *Have I considered all the questions others might ask of me in that scenario? Do I have competent answers prepared?*

As with communication skills, the key to being commercial is understanding others' needs, addressing them, speaking in a language they understand, acting as they want you to act, pre-empting their problems with your solutions (not necessarily the right solutions) and showing a common-sense interest in the affairs of your end-user. It is also about being human, appearing relaxed and laughing at yourself occasionally, whilst reflecting a sense of urgency when it is needed and called for.

If you are not doing this then you will find that potential investors in you, internal and external, will declare themselves 'out' rather quickly. The difference in a law firm (as compared with the BBC) is that they will not tell you they are out, it will not be as glamorous or exciting, and you will end up feeling like a leper. In short, your potential investors will not speak to you much anymore ...

DISPLAYING A COMMERCIAL APPROACH TO THOSE YOU WORK WITH WHEN STARTING OUT

Let's keep this simple. Acting commercially involves understanding several, key elements. Conveniently, they are all linked to words that start with the letter 'P', as follows:

Peston — As BBC News Business Editor, Robert Peston was the chap who broke the Northern Rock scoop when the economic downturn began. And, for a business affairs journalist, he writes engagingly, insightfully and (this is the key) with a broad, fun, non-intellectually snobby appeal. You should read his blog on the BBC website whenever you can; it's a great way to understand macro-economic issues in an accessible way. Whilst some have criticised Robert for dumbing down sophisticated economic theory, most of his critics are just jealous of his success. Robert is a great business communicator and exponent of what we like to call 'the intelligent mother' test – a test you should apply regularly to your own professional activities at work.

The Intelligent Mother Test

My mother is a highly intelligent woman. She understands complex concepts and theories because she is bright and thoughtful. However, she is not a lawyer. She, therefore, would not understand obscure legal jargon (nor would she want to). If you are wondering whether you are being commercial in your communication (when, for example, delivering research to a non-lawyer), ask yourself whether your mother would understand what you are saying. If the answer is no, you are not speaking in commercial terms but in pompous legal-eagle terms.

Top Tip

If you quote law in any context, you always need to explain its relevance to business and how that will directly affect your client (whether internal or external). Failure to do this will frustrate those with whom you work and will, ultimately, hinder your embryonic career.

Process — The onus is on you, when you start out as a solicitor, to become a 'process specialist'. What does this mean? It means having a system for everything you do. Also, being appropriately transparent so that those around you can see you are organised and in control. Transparency should be 'appropriate' because the obligation is always on you to establish, appreciate and understand the working patterns and preferences of those with whom you sit or come across at work, and to adapt accordingly. This means generally doing the following:

- Train yourself up in **Microsoft Excel** and become a spreadsheet guru. Senior lawyers are generally terrible at spreadsheets. You can stand out. To do so you must embrace your inner-geek and have a spreadsheet for everything that might require it (and occasionally things that do not). Encourage others to use your spreadsheets, and offer to create spreadsheets for them if appropriate. Retain control of the file so that everyone knows you created it; big brownie points ...

- Develop brilliant **PowerPoint skills** and, again, always be in charge of the slide presentation document where appropriate. Lawyers love PowerPoint. Always offer to create a first draft of a presentation before someone else gets in and does it. Apply the PowerPoint best practice guidelines set out in chapter six. Go the extra mile. It will be appreciated, even if that appreciation isn't articulated directly to you.

- Always offer to be in control of things others do not necessarily want to control. At completion of a deal, for example, be the one who offers to keep tabs on documents (drafts/final versions/who signs what/ key dates/outstanding issues) and set up a system for letting people know what is required of them in the lead-up to that all-important completion meeting. Manage the key and/or ancillary documents, manage a key element of the deal!

- Take charge of regular catch-ups with all your various 'teams'. Volunteer to set up team meetings and send calendar requests to attendees from your diary. Having your name as the 'meeting organiser' in the request is both empowering and profile-enhancing.

- Have a simple system for keeping your team or mini-team updated regarding your clients' affairs and business. Try using the 'Google Alert' system (you enter a 'keyword' into Google – eg your client's name – and you will receive a report each day with links to all the Internet news items that relate to that issue/word), and then circulating your report each week or as appropriate (ask the senior partner what suits).

- Always give as much information as possible when briefing others in any context. If you send an e-mail, always attach relevant documents in soft copy for reference, with an offer to provide hard copies if appropriate.

- Never send a blank meeting request to anyone. Always insert a tailored 'blurb' explaining the relevance and reason for the meeting. Cryptic, empty meeting requests annoy everyone in law firms.

- Always consider resourcing. In every context. Before suggesting anything, always ask yourself *'How will that work in practice?'*. If you can't visualise a credible, pragmatic answer, don't suggest a solution.

Constructive ideas are great; empty ideas are pointless. You are not an advertising executive with an unlimited budget.

Projection — Commercial people project an ability to 'do' business. They look sharp, credible and, largely, formal — especially when they are starting out in a fledgling business career (like you). This is even more important when working as a junior in a commercial law firm.

Consequently, for the first two years of your career (either as a trainee and/ or as an NQ), err on the smarter side of business-dress. Wear a tie most days and to all meetings (regardless of venue) if you are a man, and wear a proper suit if you are a woman (following the same rules regarding meetings), so that you can be taken anywhere, anytime, without it being awkward or time-consuming for you or your seniors.

Ask yourself, when you get dressed before work, '*Do I look **trendy and relaxed**, or **professional and credible?**'*. When starting out, the latter should be the norm. The former should happen only when others more senior than you dress like that. And even then, never in your office during working hours or in the offices of a client.

- *Men*: keep obvious labels for nightclubs and go easy on hair gel or wax. There is a fine line between young, fashion-conscious lawyer on his way to a client meeting, and an irritating estate agent from Essex on his way to 'Innuendo' nightclub in Chigwell after work. And don't ever undo the top button of your shirt to reveal a forest of chest hair (to show you are 'relaxed') at work. Never wear short-sleeved shirts. Ever.

- *Women*: when putting on make-up, consider whether you want people to notice it. Do you want to be identified by others as '*the Umpa-lumpa sitting in the corner wearing too much slap*', or as '*the smart trainee/associate taking notes in the meeting*'. Also consider whether the height of your heels will impede your ability to walk fast or carry things for your supervisor/seniors on the way to meetings or around the office.

Personal touch — Linked to communication skills, commercial relationships are built face-to-face and not via e-mail. Face-to-face is the only way to make people like and trust you when they first meet you.

Therefore, always consider picking up the phone to discuss something and following it up in writing, rather than simply firing off a lengthy e-mail or dictated letter. Always warn someone before sending a letter or e-mail with scores of attachments. When chatting on the phone, mirror the way your recipient communicates with you, but go with a presumption of formality to begin with until you have a good understanding of the recipient's style. Always use professional language — never use words that denote extremes of emotion (eg 'angry'/'irritated'/'upset') or suggest that you're a bit thick (eg 'confused'/'baffled'/'scrambled'), which can also suggest passive-aggression to your recipient.

Present — Commercial business people are good presenters. Not necessarily hilarious performers, but great presenters. Why? Because they plan everything they say to ensure confidence. In doing this, they are able to make their spoken advice engaging, insightful and (get ready for it …) fun, not funny! So, as a young, commercial, bright thing, you should offer to present wherever possible and follow the advice in chapter six on presentation skills. Get as much practice as possible early on in your career. That piece of research you just did - can you present your findings to your workgroup for five minutes? That trainee induction session on Monday — can you speak about your experience as a trainee to the others to add context? Take responsibility for finding opportunities to maximise your exposure in your department and firm. It will pay dividends. The key to this is forging good relationships with your knowledge management lawyers, Professional Development or Professional Support Lawyers (PDLs or PSLs, if you have them) or taking responsibility for your department's know-how if you don't.

Profit — always think of the profit you add to everything you do. What stamp have you put on a piece of work? What makes it your piece of work? And – this is key – how are you delivering work? Some use the phrase '*under-promise and over-deliver*' in business. Never fool yourself into thinking that this approach will work with your senior colleagues when you are a junior lawyer. It is much more important that you are a safe pair of hands. If you under-promise, they will think you are unambitious and unwilling to 'go the extra mile' to get the job done. If you then over-deliver on that promise, they will think you are unable to manage your time properly and that you are incapable of giving a sensible estimate. And if you have spent time doing things they did not ask you to do, they might not thank you. They did not, after all, ask you to do them. And now, they have to waste their time writing off your 'extra' time.

So, should you ever go the extra mile? Yes — but just say you are going to do it before you do the job, not afterwards (ie at the delegating and planning stage). Business people do not generally like surprises. Even good ones. And this applies both internally and externally. Internally, because your senior colleagues do not like to be shown up by young upstarts; and externally because clients do not like surprises that might cost them money.

In fact you should never surprise a client as a junior lawyer — it is not your job. However, offering 'profit' and the 'extra mile' at the planning stage gives your colleagues or clients the opportunity to say 'No thanks'. That is win–win for you, because:

a) you have shown initiative in the planning of your job and the added 'value' you have offered. They can take up your offer or refuse it;

b) they feel that you are interested in thinking laterally and not just as a lawyer;

c) they feel like they are in control and that they retain ownership of the direction in which you are heading with regard to that piece of work;

d) you do not waste your time doing things for which no one will thank you; morale intact!

What should the phrase 'under-promise, over-deliver' be? Perhaps:

Promise to achieve what they want you to achieve when they ask you to do something and offer your well thought-through ideas as to how extra might be added, agree the plan of action and then deliver what you agreed to deliver on time, on budget and on topic; no more, no less.

Agreed, the phrase is not as neat, but it is far more accurate.

To achieve this, the key is to ask the right questions when you receive work. Questions like:

- *Can you tell me a bit about the matter/transaction/case before we move onto the work in which you would like to involve me?*

- *What are the commercial drivers behind the matter/transaction/case?*

- *When is this going out?*

- *Do you have a starting point in mind?*

- *How long do you envisage this taking me?*

- *Do we have a projected budget for this piece of work?*

- *Is there anything you do not want me to focus on?*

- *Does this need to be in a format to go straight out to the client?*

- *Are there any specific/separate tasks questions you would like addressed when I do this work?*

- *Are there any relevant contacts for this work?*

- *How would you like me to keep you in the loop as I progress through the work?*

- *Who are the internal team members on this matter/transaction/case?*

- *What is the matter number and time-code?*

Pretty — Always look keen, interested and available. Remember that none of your senior colleagues will remember to invite you to meetings. You are not top of their list of priorities. They would much rather just go along to the said meeting on their own, and then give you the work afterwards without explaining why. Low effort for them, but this will do nothing for either your brand or your morale. So, if you are doing a discrete piece of work for someone, always ask to go along to any meetings they attend or chair on that matter (internal and external). Remember, if you don't ask, you don't get!

Profile — Time permitting, go along to as many internal departmental meetings and training sessions (not just your own), and to as many firm-wide initiative meetings (eg, CSR) as possible. Try to aim for two a week. Go by yourself, sit next to any friendly/senior-looking people you haven't met before, introduce yourself and tell them it was really good to meet them. Next time you have a simple query that is relevant to their department or workgroup, massage their egos by pinging an e-mail across that they can answer in less than 30 seconds. Make it simple so they do not incur client time in answering it, but complex enough to be something only they could know. Do this relatively regularly and you will soon build up rapport with influential people, and a nice little business network to go with it. It will come in handy when you need urgent, cross-departmental support later down the line.

Pragmatic — It's time to ditch the faff. No one likes a faffy, waffly or moany lawyer. So, remember:

a) Don't complain about work to anyone. Save it for your appraisals or for your mentor. Even then, think very carefully about how you phrase your 'gripes'.

b) Always have facts and figures to back up any statements you make, opinions you have or assertions you put forward on a matter. Never 'go with your gut instinct' or use the phrases 'gut feeling', 'I reckon', 'I think' or 'I hope so … ' at work. Always visit your 'process' before embarking on any project and take time to plan everything, no matter how small, and offer your thought-processes to those with whom you work.

c) When phoning a fellow lawyer to discuss a work matter, always start the conversation with:

'Have you got two minutes?' — *if your query will take **less than five** minutes to discuss; or*

'Do you have a few minutes' — *if your query will take **longer than five** minutes but no more than 10 minutes to discuss; or*

'Do you have some time to discuss a matter with me. It should take about [   ] minutes. If not now, when might be convenient?'

If your query is an open-ended one and you are not sure how long it will take to discuss, be sure you keep checking back with your fellow lawyer as to time throughout your conversation, to avoid frustrating them.

d) Remember that many will judge how good you are when you are starting out by how many basic errors you make — errors you need not have made had you focused a little more on the wood than the trees. To avoid basic errors in documents, always copy and paste text you are proof-reading into another document to change the layout on your page. Then print it out and proof-read a hard copy. Never proof-read on a computer screen. Your eyes do not react efficiently to the flickering screen for long periods. It can also send you cross-eyed (not a good look at work).

Passionate — Carve a niche for yourself. In life, passionate people are attractive people. Passion is catchy. It rubs off on others. The same is true at work in a law firm; as long as the passion is not misplaced (people will ostracise you if you claim that you *'just love, love, love filling in Companies House forms'*).

So, consider the following:

As a trainee:

If you are interested in, for example, intellectual property (IP), become knowledgeable and show your passion for the area. Subscribe to the journals, keep them on your shelves so your supervisor can see, attend IP group meetings wherever possible and try to get involved in writing some articles on the subject. Do not, however, bang on about it so often that your non-IP supervisor thinks you are a one-trick pony. That will not help you when you realise that there are no jobs going in IP at qualification time.

As an NQ:

It is to be hoped you are working in a department you wanted to qualify into. So, show commitment to it. If you are good at something, exploit it. Let it become part of your brand. Keep developing yourself in other areas to build your general competence, but do not be afraid of demonstrating a clear preference for a particular direction. And use passionate language appropriately, eg 'I love contentious IP work, especially on the technology side — I've recently done some work with Google and I loved their approach to branding …' makes you sound dynamic, business-minded and interesting, not obsessed, boring and over-legal.

Generally

You should aim to read three industry-specific journals (available through your library resources) per week. Think laterally about where you might find (legal) insiders' information. For example, read as many Accountants' Reports and Information Memoranda as you can on transactional matters. You will need to understand these to carry out a junior role as a lawyer, and they are a great way to understand business issues. Remember, accounting issues more than legal ones often drive most deals!

Buy friends in different industries a drink once a month, and ask them to download and tell you everything they know about current trends, recent developments and key issues facing them as business people in their specific industries. This will help develop your business acumen, and you will get inside information to which your legal colleagues simply will not have access.

Papers and press — Read a broadsheet newspaper every day. That means a **proper** newspaper. As interesting as it is to read about 'Nelly the kitten from Bakewell and her amazing ability to peel oranges with her tail' as a double-page spread in the *Daily Mail*, it is not going to help increase your commercial edge.

Having said that, being commercial is not just about discussing finance and commerce. It is about having opinions on the issues of the day, from the latest Cabinet reshuffle to the Chancellor's Pre-Budget Report, Iranian nuclear armament and who won the men's 100 metre sprint at the Olympics. It certainly isn't about being able to discuss case law. That might be useful for a departmental know-how session, but it won't do for a client meeting. Not at all.

Read the Saturday or Sunday papers every weekend without fail (paying close attention to the business, money and finance sections in particular). Note down any stories that mention the industry in which you work or the clients with whom you work, and keep your notes in a file for later reference. Make this visible in your office to those with whom you work, and mention interesting and relevant articles occasionally to colleagues.

Read *Private Eye* for a less earnest opinion on current affairs. Also read *The Week* when you can — it's great if you need to catch up quickly on recent events (eg when returning from holiday). Spend 20 minutes a week reading the *Lawyer* (website or hard copy if you can get one!) and *Legal Week*, and perusing *rollonfriday.com*. Your senior colleagues love to discuss their industry and related gossip. You need to play the game.

What about the Financial Times? The *Financial Times* (FT) has two main purposes:

a) A useful but pretentious way to show off your financial 'sophistication' to others on public transport (if you complete the FT crossword in front of others, extra kudos points are available).

b) A rather long-winded and unnecessarily turgidly-written briefing tool for those who work in business who need to find out how money moulds their landscape daily.

Certain people love the FT, and you might well find that there are ubiquitous copies of it floating around your law firm. You might feel obliged to take one. You might feel obliged to carry one to the toilet in the morning. Worse, you might feel duty-bound to keep one next to your bed, and even buy one in an airport before going on holiday to show willing. Don't do any of the above. The FT is quite boring (it's even pink to try to make it look a little bit more 'interesting'). Given that you need to acquire only a macro- and not a micro-economic knowledge as a lawyer, there are only a few bits and bobs in the FT that are of any use to you as a legal practitioner (bits you can probably find in your daily broadsheet, albeit written with slightly more polemic).

You should aim to 'read' the FT three times per week, and whilst we recommend that you keep a copy on your desk every now and then to show willing, here is our very short, pragmatic guide to 'skim-reading' the FT:

1. Read the companies and markets section — read this first (and possibly last if you are pushed for time).

2. Read the Lex column:

    It is on the back page of the main section
    Written by the FT's bright young things
    It is read by chief executives, bankers and lawyers
    It is a great way of detecting the trading patterns of companies

And then stop.

Top Tips

Set out on the page opposite are some top tips for juniors attending external meetings (or internal meetings with external clients):

External Meetings

- Take copies for everyone of everything and anything that is relevant. Be the document organiser — it is commercial and it communicates uber-efficiency. If you have time, make a tabulated document bundle and ok it with your supervisor/boss to see if he/she has anything to add before the meeting. This will impress external clients no end, and will show your supervisor/boss you think ahead logically.

- Offer to speak on work you (specifically) have undertaken. Put a simple question to your supervisor/boss, like *'I know we are due to discuss some advice in relation to that piece of research I did the other day. Would it be useful if I quickly summarised the key issues for the client at some point in the meeting?'*. This shows that you can take the initiative, that you are keen and that you want to build a positive brand for yourself. It is also high visibility.

- If you are due to present something formally in a meeting, be guided by your supervisor/boss as to how best this might be communicated to attendees (format and style). You do not want to go on for too long (time is money), and you do not want to turn up brandishing 50 PowerPoint slides and a laminated handout when you were meant to speak for only two minutes. Be savvy, draft a plan and discuss it with your supervisor/boss before embarking on the work.

- Be on time — even if your boss is not. Offer to go on ahead of him/her if he/she is running late. 'Face-time' like this is a great opportunity to build rapport, strike up conversation and build bridges with meeting attendees.

- Prepare your introduction as follows:
  Hi, I am [NAME], I work with [NAME OF PARTNER/SUPERVISOR] on [FILE MATTER/PROJECT], specifically on the [YOUR ELEMENT OF THE FILE/ MATTER/PROJECT]. Here is my business card in case you need get in touch with me after this meeting.

- If you are taking a note, make sure you swap business cards with all attendees. Tell your supervisor/boss you are going to do this before the meeting. If your supervisor/boss objects then do not do it, but the chances are that this will be fine. After all, there is nothing wrong with asking attendees for contact information; it is common sense. The physical act of taking the card from another helps to cement that person's face and name in your brain, so that you can take effective notes, remembering who is speaking without having to make up ridiculous nick-names (eg Baldy/Speckie/Big Nose) to keep up.

- Throughout the meeting, try not to sit too far away from your supervisor or the person leading the meeting, otherwise you will be perceived as nothing more than a note-taking scribe. If your supervisor/boss tells you where to sit and you are worried you might feel marginalised, ask if you can sit a little closer, explaining that it will help you take an accurate note. Interject appropriately to show others what you are doing, eg 'That sounded important, can I just make sure I recorded that correctly?'

- If you need the toilet during a meeting, go. You are not at primary school. Gesture to your supervisor/boss that you need to go so that he/she knows you will not be taking notes for the next few minutes. Make sure you make eye contact with him/her before leaving. Do not just slip out. In any event, there is a good chance your supervisor/boss will need to go as well and will take the opportunity to adjourn the meeting for a few minutes so everyone can take a short break. Those biscuits won't eat themselves …

- After the meeting, offer to be the one who drafts and sends out the follow-up e-mail summarising the discussion and relevant action points. Getting your e-mail address into the e-address books of all attendees is a good profile-builder and sends a simple message of credibility.

- Enjoy meetings — many would say that they are the best bit of the job!

COMMERCIALITY TOP TIPS SUMMARY

- Remember, knowing what a specific share is doing on the NASDAQ on any particular day does not mean you are being 'commercial'. Commerciality is about showing those around you that you are interested in the world of business and are able to discuss all the issues that affect the way you deal with clients as a legal adviser. Remember, you are not an economist.

- Have a well-considered process for everything you do. Review and evaluate that process at the end of every major piece of work you do.

- Never express an opinion or make a statement without having the facts and figures to back it up. Never go with your gut ...

- Make sure you are up to speed on the major socio-political issues of the day. Commercial lawyers have articulate opinions on all kinds of things that affect us as human beings.

- Never do a piece of work without asking for context first.

- Always follow up after doing a discrete piece of work on a matter.

- Always send an e-mail after every meeting you have, summarising the conclusions and action points.

- Make sure you have a copy of the FT visible on your desk for others to see three times a week.

- Read a broadsheet newspaper every day, three industry-specific journals every week and the papers once on the weekend (with a focus on the business section or supplement).

- Attend as many cross-departmental meetings as possible to build your business network.

6

Be Visible – Demystifying Legal Presentation Skills

In the 1980s, a presentation at work in a commercial organisation meant 63 acetate sheets, an overhead projector, a script learnt verbatim to minimise the risk of mistakes, and some 'Blue Ribbon' biscuits at half-time, with some milky Nescafé in a polystyrene cup and a crafty cigarette in the toilets. No one expected 'razzmatazz' and no real significance was placed upon being able to present with style in the workplace or in front of clients. In law firms, wowing those who paid the fees simply meant producing water-tight legal documents, sealing the deal at 3am, taking the team out for an over-priced Beef Wellington and a bottle of Taittinger, and then billing and recovering promptly. Job done.

In the twenty-first century, successful, modern solicitors (at all levels of seniority) are good at presentations. Part of their positive personal brand is the ability to speak with charisma, to make complex information appear simple, to make dull information appear interesting and to make heavy information appear light – not light-weight, just light in tone. Such solicitors make a huge impact on others by getting up (or sitting down...) and presenting. Clients — internal and external — see it as a huge asset to have a competent presenter on their team. Many believe that having good presentation skills is a basic requirement for the job these days. Being a people person is now essential, not just desirable. A great way to show that you are a likeable, charming and confident 'people person' is by presenting well when it is needed.

For some reason, however, presentation skills have acquired an aura of mystery over the years. Many believe, or want to believe, that there is some kind of magic to presenting, that you either are a presenter or you are not, and that effective presenting involves giving a performance in front of colleagues. This is utter rubbish. There is nothing to fear.

Why? Because effective presenting is about preparation. As a lawyer (at whatever level), you will be very good at preparing and planning for things. It's one of your core skills: reducing risk by covering bases and blocking the exits. It makes you tick and gives you satisfaction. It should come as no surprise to you, therefore, that the people who present best are the ones who prepare most effectively and appropriately.

I HATE PERFORMING …

No one is expecting you to perform like Richard Burton, to speak like Barack Obama or to amuse like Eddie Izzard. That should not be your concern. What people are expecting is that you have planned and prepared for your presentation meticulously. After all, a lawyer who cannot prepare properly is like a sniper who can't shoot. Useless. And remember, you are delivering a presentation as a lawyer! Your audience will invariably have rather low expectations before you start. If you do an average job, therefore, you will be doing well in their eyes; a good job and you will be excellent; and if you do a brilliant job, you will be truly outstanding.

With the above in mind, remember the following as you sequence through this chapter:

a) No one ever presents at work unless there is a business need for it. If someone has asked you to deliver a presentation, the audience will invariably be on your side.

b) If you give your audience useful information that is relevant to their jobs in an engaging way, they won't notice if you shift about a bit and look a little nervous (you're a lawyer, not an actor!).

c) If you show that you are interested in what the members of your audience think, and that you have thought about their needs at the planning stage, you will win.

d) The 'performance' aspect of your presentation comprises only 15 per cent of the impact you can make when you get up in front of colleagues or external clients. This is because if you plan and prepare fully and start confidently, your delivery will naturally be more relaxed and light-hearted.

At the risk of repetition, the only reason almost anyone ever delivers a poor presentation is because that person has not prepared enough, or has prepared in the wrong way.

TRAINING VERSUS PRESENTING?

To keep things simple, everything in this chapter will work if you are delivering either a training session or a presentation in your capacity as a lawyer and/ or subject-matter expert, in any context. Why? Because great training and great presenting is all about preparing in the right way and engaging with your audience in an empathetic manner. With this in mind, there really is no difference between a cracking presentation and a truly memorable training session at your level. Let's examine how this might be achieved ...

The successful presenting ladder

Each step of the presenting ladder builds momentum towards a truly excellent presentation. How?

• CAREFUL PLANNING AND PREPARATION generates

Careful Planning + Prep generates:

- DEEP CONFIDENCE WITH PRESENTATION MATERIAL/SUBJECT-MATTER which means you have

- LESS FEAR OF YOUR AUDIENCE CATCHING YOU OUT which helps you

- INTERACT WITH YOUR AUDIENCE which helps your

- AUDIENCE RELAX which in turn helps

- YOU RELAX and shed your negative self-consciousness.

It will come as no surprise, therefore, that this chapter will focus more heavily on the planning and preparation elements of your presentation than anything else.

Worry not, we'll have a decent look at the 'in the room' or performance skills associated with presenting, including how you might use PowerPoint, flipcharts and handouts to enhance your presentation, later in this chapter.

A STRUCTURE FOR THIS CHAPTER

The rest of this chapter has been divided into the following numbered sections, to guide you through the process of planning and executing your presentation:

1. Why should you present?

2. What is a legal presentation?

3. Getting started

4. Planning my presentation – the needs of my audience

5. A clear structure

6. Interactivity – what works best?

7. Handling challenging questions in legal presentations

8. Using crib-notes

9. Humour and the funnies ...

1. WHY SHOULD YOU PRESENT?

As we know, competition in the legal landscape is now more intense than ever. And this competition exists at every 'legal' level:

- Between law firms to acquire the best clients and the most 'high-profile' work, and also to win awards/accolades.

- Between departments within law firms to show the most productivity.

- Between lawyers to get promotions and meet aspirational goals.

This means ...

On a macro-scale: Your firm has to work really hard to carve a niche for itself in a market that is increasingly saturated with law firms that all claim to be individual, client-focused, market-leading and innovative.

On a micro-scale: You have to work really hard to give yourself a unique selling point ('USP') internally, to stand out and to make yourself irreplaceable to your firm, peers and colleagues.

Presenting effectively and professionally is a key element of this USP.

2. WHAT IS A LEGAL PRESENTATION?

In many ways, you are making a presentation every time you interact with someone in a professional context, whom you need to impress. With this in mind, there are three types of presentations:

Informal — One-to-one report/feedback/briefings (even walking into a senior colleague's office to report back on a simple piece of research).

Formal — Group presentations, pitches and training sessions, either standing up or sitting down in front of people who are listening to and watching you present for a defined period of time.

Conferences — Presenting information to large groups in large rooms, often behind a lectern. We're not going to focus our specific attention on this format in this chapter as it's unlikely you will spend a lot of time engaged in this activity as a junior commercial lawyer.

The irony is that so-called 'informal' presentations (eg walking into a partner's room to deliver your research) can become the most formal of all, given the intensity of their 'one-on-one' dynamic.

Forget the performance ...

Presenting is about having the right attitude, not about what you wear and how you look (although that contributes).

It is not about 'performing'. In fact, sometimes easy merit points can be won simply by designing a session or presentation for someone else to deliver. Just think how impressive you would look in the following circumstances:

- **Internal client (Partner A)** has been asked to present at a conference next week and is away on business until then. If things go well, there will be some good work as a result of it. Despite being very busy, you offer to prepare the presentation. Partner A takes you along to the conference for experience and exposure. At the conference, she introduces you to various contacts and you end up as that partner's number two on the work that comes through as a result.

- **External client (Commercial Director B)** has been asked to present to his Board on a non-legal, strategic business issue next Tuesday, and he is panicking. He hates presenting. You take the time to prepare a presentation for him to deliver at that meeting and talk him through it for no charge; he looks great in front of his colleagues and you've a made a best friend for life. Next time this happens, you get a personal invitation to attend the Board meeting.

If you find yourself designing a presentation, session or workshop for someone else, it is just as important, perhaps even more important, that you make sure they feel (and are!) prepared, comfortable and fully briefed.

When should I deliver a presentation?

Whenever you can. Presentations at work may be delivered for a number of reasons — all related to the business of your law firm: to update, to brief, to inform, to educate, to motivate, to turn negative (a mistake was made) into positive (that mistake won't happen again) and – believe it or not – for sheer enjoyment.

The onus is on you to think laterally about how a presentation you could deliver might benefit the business in some, tangible way and get you noticed for the right reasons. Some examples might be as follows:

- You have just done some research into a useful piece of law and there is a team meeting tomorrow morning. *Offer to do five minutes on it at the end.*

- You are in department A and you have just completed a cross-departmental deal. You now think department B might benefit from a briefing/update. *Speak to the partner in charge and get something in the diary.*

- You are involved in a new procedure for reviewing contracts/putting together witness statements that might benefit your colleagues. *Get a room and talk your colleagues through it, and get them to have a go.*

- Your team made a mistake on a matter and you need to point out the risk issues to others working in that area. *Deliver a training session.*

- Your client does not know your team and how it functions. *You offer to attend at the client's offices and deliver an introductory briefing.*

Understanding the goals ...

As mentioned above, at your level you don't need to worry about the difference between presenting and training. A good presentation should have clear learning goals ('objectives') and benefits ('outcomes') for the attendees, otherwise what's the point? An effective training session should have the same goals and benefits. Training should be provided only when there is a tangible business need for it. Likewise, a presentation should be delivered only when there is a clear requirement for one.

The potential pitfall for legal practitioners lies in their risk-averse nature. If a lawyer believes a group of people needs to know certain things, the temptation might be to stand behind a lectern and talk in front of a voluminous PowerPoint slideshow until he/she is happy that the risk has been transferred to the audience. That way, there is no risk of humiliation, the risk 'box' has been ticked and the job has been done.

Do this at your own peril. It is a short-term and dangerous strategy for someone at your level. If you take one thing away from this chapter, it's that **the more important the information you are trying to convey in a presentation, the more important it is to engage your participants in some way**.

Presentations are not lectures. Lectures take place at university. And at university, lectures took place at awkward times (first thing in the morning before you'd woken up properly, just after lunch in the blood-sugar meltdown zone, or last thing in the day when you were tired and wanted to go home or out to relax with friends), under low-lighting and were invariably delivered by someone with a catastrophically soporific voice. For some students, this often led to sleep — deep sleep — with no learning benefit whatsoever. And how much did you remember if you didn't take copious notes? Almost nothing.

To achieve maximum impact, therefore, any presentation you deliver at work should be more workshop than lecture, more engaging and interactive than 'teachery', and memorable specifically for your delivery and facilitation.

Contrary to popular belief, any session whatsoever (and that includes the driest legal-technical topic) can involve audience engagement and participation in some form, no matter how small. The challenge is to make the leap of faith, using a few simple techniques, and trust that your audience will want to interact if you plan well and present with confidence.

3. GETTING STARTED

Despite what you might think, very few people in life speak publicly 'off the cuff.' This is because genuinely wonderful presenters leave no stone unturned in preparing for their big moment. That gives them the freedom to play with their plan on the day, and to make changes if necessary at the last minute. However, such changes are low-risk because each stage of their presentation has been strategised. Where and how did they start?

A common presenting scenario
It is Friday. You have just finished a huge piece of research into a new statutory provision and its regulatory effect on the legal landscape and, specifically, the structure of the deal your team is working on. The partner you report to has asked you to deliver a briefing presentation to the team (12 lawyers) next week over lunch. You have 40 minutes. This is a great opportunity to achieve profile in front of the team.

First steps ...

Let's begin with a few things you should not do:

a) Start dumping information into a PowerPoint presentation, create handouts and see how it flows once I've come up with some ideas on slides. Surely I can just talk around what I produce ... ?

b) Improvise. I know this piece of law back-to-front now; I could speak on it for hours. We will do a Q&A and then I can just chat with attendees.

c) Read out my research findings for half an hour, finish early and get out as quickly as possible because I hate presenting and my subject-matter bores me.

Adopting any of the above approaches will result in a presentation disaster. Avoid this by taking the following steps.

4. PLANNING MY PRESENTATION – THE NEEDS OF MY AUDIENCE

Whether it is a one-to-one or group presentation, your first consideration before writing any presentation should be to consider the needs and requirements of your audience. Just like communicating with impact and displaying a sense of commerciality, to deliver a great presentation you have to focus on what your **customer** wants.

What your audience **expects** from you may appear obvious. If you are asked to give a talk on the law of contract interpretation, the audience might expect to be given a detailed overview of the current thinking in the courts.

But is this what they really **want**? Chances are, if you are giving a presentation on the law, what the audience wants may comprise a combination of the following:

- Some kind of overview of the current thinking of the courts.

- To get the necessary Continuing Professional Development (CPD) points for the current year.

- To obtain a decent, free lunch.

- To understand enough about recent case law so that they can deal with difficult client questions.

- To understand enough about recent case law so that they can draft the provision of the contract to which this area relates.

What the audience also probably **needs** includes the following:

- To be comfortable.

- To be back at their desks by Xpm, when they were told the presentation would end.

- Not be kept too long without a break, or something to eat or drink.

- For the talk not to be too complicated or turgid.

- For the talk not to be boring.

- For you to be clear, loud enough to hear and not to stand in the way of your slides, if you choose to use slides (which you probably shouldn't).

- To be able to understand the information they receive.

- To be able to remember the key points accurately when they are faced with difficult questions on the subject matter in their daily practice.

- To remember the talk and you as the presenter.

To **meet and exceed your audience's expectations**, before creating your presentation you should ask yourself questions such as:

- Who are my audience?

- How senior are they?

- How many are they?

- How will they be sitting? Cinema-style, or boardroom-style seating?

- What is their existing knowledge?

- Will I have to acknowledge differing levels of expertise to avoid patronising those who are already knowledgeable?

You should then take a piece of A4 paper and answer the following questions (in writing):

1. *What is the topic?*

2. *How long have you got?*

3. *Who asked you do deliver this presentation?*

4. *Why did they ask you to deliver this presentation?*

5. *What deadlines are there? (These should be your own (false) deadline and the real (imposed) deadline.)*

6.   *What do you think you should cover?*

7.   *What is/are the attendee(s) hoping to get out of it?*

8.   *How will the **business** benefit from this presentation?*

9.   *What do the attendees **not** need to know, ie what information is of no interest or consequence to them?*

10.   *Where can your attendees find more information on the topic?*

Do this well and you will have the structural basis for a great presentation.

How?

The questions numbered **6 and 7** (and also 8) are key here. These are the **OBJECTIVES** (6) and **OUTCOMES** (7). Note that question 8 is forcing you to think about the **COMMERCIAL CONSEQUENCES** of your presentation.

The best presenters make sure that their objectives are aligned with their outcomes. For example:

OBJECTIVE: I want to cover the scope of House of Lords decision X.

OUTCOME: I want attendees to come away with an understanding of the steps needed to incorporate this new law into their day-to-day procedural activities, or in non-legal speak when they have to explain it to a client.

Taking time to consider question **9** will also help to focus your mind. Be as concise as you possibly can, so that you don't waste time and risk frustrating your audience with useless (or indirectly relevant) information.

Understanding how you are going to address **question 8** is vital. **What change in behaviour or increase in knowledge are you looking to effect at work as a result of your presentation?** Once you know this, you will be better placed to understand what material you need to cover and in how much depth. Ask yourself the following:

- *What should my audience be able to do after the presentation that they were not able to do before? Specifically, after seeing you talk, what will they be able to do:*

- *Straight after the session?*

- *In one week?*

- *In one month?*

- *In six months?*

- *... that they couldn't do before?*

You can even give your audience this information when you start your presentation! It shows forethought, planning and a real business focus.

More than you can chew

One of the biggest mistakes lawyers make when they present is to try to present too much. Remember, no one will mind if you finish your presentation early. Everyone will mind if you finish late. Be realistic. Can you really cover the law of Tort in 15 minutes? Can you really cover Part 36 Offers under the CPR in 10 minutes?

The *'ratio'* of your presentation

All good presentations have what we call a **Hallway Message**. This is the **key business message** that pervades your presentation. Fundamentally, it is the one thing that people will remember about the presentation when they leave the room, even if they remember nothing else.

In legal terms, the Hallway Message is the '**essence**' of your presentation. It is a very succinct summary of your presentation, clear in your own head and easily communicable at the end of your presentation, for your attendees to take away and pass on to others during a quick conversation in an office hallway.

It is raised here because you need to be clear in your own mind as to what your specific Hallway Message is **before** writing your presentation (although it will not be revealed until the end of your presentation. We'll examine this later on).

5. A CLEAR STRUCTURE

Now that you have planned your presentation, you need to add a structure to it. Some people believe presentations should be structured in much the same way as essays were at school, namely:

- Tell 'em what you're going to say
- Tell 'em
- Tell 'em what you've said

Or, in other words:

- Introduction
- Main body
- Conclusion

This methodology is wrong for a legal presentation. Why? Because when adopted by verbose and sometimes slightly self-important lawyers, this all too often turns into:

- Introduction
- Main bit one
- Interim conclusion
- Main bit two
- Interim conclusion
- Main bit three
- Interim conclusion

- Return to introduction

- Repeating main bits

- Conclusion and repeating a bit more you forgot to mention earlier

- Whoops, I've overrun and that one in the corner appears to have fallen into a boredom-induced coma

- Rush to finish and miss key information

- Repeat conclusion

- Finish, embarrassed ... must leave without making eye contact

Rather, use the following structure:

A. The Opener

B. The Introduction

C. The Main Body

D. The Business Message/Advice

E. The Conclusion

F. Close and Thanks

Let's look at each one in turn.

A. The Opener

Your opener is about establishing **you** as a presenter; stamping your authority on your presentation from the word 'go' is crucial. You need to show the audience that you are comfortable and credible in front of them. You have to let the audience know that you have something important to tell them, and that you know how you intend to deliver it.

A confident opener will also calm your nerves, allowing you to relax into your presentation.

Your opener lasts no more than 30 seconds, is learnt verbatim, ie without notes, is delivered with engaging eye contact and covers the following:

a) Who you are (including job title and department).

b) Thanking the audience for coming.

c) Why you are there — who told you to deliver this? Why now? Why here?

d) How long you will speak for and what time you will finish.

e) Questions — you'll answer them as you go through, or take them at the end. Be clear, assertive and consistent with this. If you tell your audience you will take questions at the end, do not take them as you go through. And vice versa.

f) Acknowledge seniority levels, to avoid being accused of patronising if this is appropriate.

g) Get going!

Let's look at an example of a succinct opener delivered to a legal team by an associate, Phil, at the request of senior partner, Frank:

"(a): Good afternoon everyone. My name is Phil Mitchell, I'm an associate in the Corporate Team, private equity group. (b): Thanks for coming along. (c): Why are you all here? Well, given our collective involvement in Project Cognac, Frank Butcher asked me to report back on a piece of research I recently carried out in relation to section XXX of the Companies Act that might well affect the nature of our transaction . (d): I should be able to cover everything in an hour so, we'll be finished by 2pm.(e): If you have any questions, stick your hand up as we go through and I'll try to answer them . If we don't have time during the presentation, I'll follow-up with you afterwards . (f): Before I get going, I am aware that some of you might already know some of what I intend to cover. If this is the case, I'll look to get your input as we go through so we can bring everyone up to the same level of knowledge . (g): So, let's get going ."

What does each part do?

a) *Your professional status has been communicated, they know who are you and why they should listen to you in particular.*

b) *You show your appreciation for their time (remember, for lawyers, time means money!)*

c) *You have given them a reason to listen to what you have to say right now.*

d) *Housekeeping over, now you can move on to the nitty gritty.*

e) *This makes you look proactive and calm — if you run out of time, you can get 'face-time' with the attendees afterwards, which can mean extra brownie-points.*

f) *By saying this you will avoid anyone in the room interpreting your talk as patronising. By asking for input from those who might already know some of the material you intend to cover, you are also acknowledging differing levels of seniority and massaging egos at the same time. However, if you commit to procuring input from your audience, make sure you do so to avoid frustrating them. Depending on the seniority of your audience (eg a junior group of trainees), you might not need to employ this strategy every time.*

g) *You and your audience are now ready for business — the presentation is now starting in earnest.*

The opener is a model to adapt to your individual presentation. You might not need to include all the above elements. Think of it as a recommended menu and tailor it accordingly to suit your style. Don't, whatever you do, miss your opener out.

Now move on to the Introduction.

B. The Introduction

Having established some professional credibility with your opener, it is time to move on to the introduction.

The introduction is all about **your talk**, not you. Why should your audience listen to your presentation? Lasting no more than **two to three minutes**, your introduction should cover the following:

STEP (1)   Break the ice

Break the ice by choosing one of the following safe options:

SET THE SCENE: A common experience; something that creates a common bond between you and your audience. Why? In crudely scientific terms, people like people whom they perceive as being similar to them. With this in mind, building a bond with your audience involves showing them that you are in the same 'boat' as them in some way. This helps them feel as though you are working with them as a team and not simply showing them how knowledgeable you are. It builds rapport.

FACTS AND FIGURES: Perhaps you might open your introduction with some relevant facts and figures? Perhaps they are shocking? Perhaps they are amusing? Perhaps they're simply surprising? Whatever they are, they are genuine and they grab the attention of your audience to help them understand the salience to their day-to-day professional lives of your presentation.

INTERACTIVITY: Showing your audience you are happy to engage with them at the start of your presentation is a great way to get 'buy-in' from them from the outset. It doesn't need to be earth-shattering — something light and non-humiliating for you and/or your audience works very well; a show of hands or a vote works perfectly, as long as you tie it in to your talk (see the 'interactivity options' box later in this chapter).

Slightly more high-risk is to ask your audience what they are hoping to cover in your session (putting the input on a flipchart or equivalent as a 'guide' or 'ticklist' for your presentation). Despite the risk, the benefit of audience interaction at the start of your presentation is that it helps to make you **appear** relaxed, natural and spontaneous, even if you are not!

STEP (2)   Communicate your objectives

Explain what you intend to cover, in what order and why.

STEP (3)   Communicate your outcomes

Tell the attendees what they should be able to do as a result of your session.

STEP (4)   Tell them that you are now moving on to your first point/ issue/section/idea

Don't faff – get on with it and move in to your main body...

C. The Main Body

Now it's time to get into the meat of your presentation. And by 'meat', we mean a fresh, classy, tasty, interesting, mouth-watering feast , not a cheap, old Turkey Twizzler.

A significant majority of legal presentations will involve the transfer of important and potentially risky information. It is therefore vital that your audience substantively remembers what you cover.

Building on the learning theory we covered in chapter four on communication skills, research shows that just watching and/or listening to information (ie visual and auditory – say, watching a PowerPoint presentation) is significantly less effective in terms of long-term embedded learning than doing, participating or experiencing (ie kinaesthetic — say, marking up a handout as you speak). So, to make a real long-term impact, great presentations cover all three learning preferences when they sequence into the main section.

Most human beings can concentrate whilst being talked at for only about 20 minutes before they start to switch off. To prevent this, you should aim to engage with your audience at least every 15 minutes during your presentation.

What does 'engage' mean? Engaging means interactivity. It means shaking things up a bit every quarter of an hour, and giving everyone in your audience the opportunity to 'engage' their brains and to experience kinaesthetic learning — learning by doing and experiencing.

This should not sound scary. Interactivity doesn't mean asking your attendees to dress as monkeys and do the hokey-kokey whilst they draft a force majeure clause. It just means showing them you care what they think; asking them to contribute, and actively and visibly valuing their input.

A collateral benefit of seeking input from your audience is that you won't be stared at silently for the duration of your session — great news if you are feeling nervous.

But there is a caveat: interactivity should not (unless you are a seasoned speaking professional, or a trainer with years of experience) be spontaneous. When you ask questions of the audience, you know the answer. When you use flipcharts, you know what is going up on the paper before you ask for input. When you ask for a show of hands, you know what to expect. When you use a case study, you have model answers prepared and ready to go. You must carefully choreograph how you might facilitate any discussion to ensure you don't go too far off-piste and off-time.

D. The Business Message/Advice

Now is the time to draw things together. You have covered the 'meat', you have interacted with your audience and you are now happy that the attendees understand the important information. Now you should tie everything back to business. In no more than five minutes, you should aim to do the following:

- Summarise how this all relates to the business and to the attendees' day-to-day jobs.

- Express an opinion and give your advice — show your ability to think laterally and insightfully. This is an opportunity to display an intellectual thought-process.

E. The Conclusion

Your conclusion and your Hallway Message must now combine to tie off and complete your presentation. In no more than one and a half minutes, you should aim to do the following:

- Summarise the outcomes, but do not repeat your objectives or your introduction.

- Deliver your Hallway Message — the succinct 'ratio' of your presentation.

- Tell your audience where to find more information and outline available resources going forward.

F. Close and Thanks

Make this section of your presentation quick and final, unless you intend to leave time to answer questions (if you do, see our handling challenging questions box on page 120).

6. INTERACTIVITY – WHAT WORKS BEST?

As we know, interacting and engaging with your audience in the main body of your presentation shows them you are not only relaxed, but also humble and interested in their opinions and ideas (an important consideration when the sharing of legal knowledge is a key risk reducer in law firms).

Table 6.1 below sets out a range of interactivity options for you to choose from when designing your talk, including examples of how and when they might be employed.

Table 6.1 *Interactivity options*

Name	Details	Example and hints	Risk
PowerPoint Handout	See below for **PowerPoint** and **Handout** best practice	See below for **PowerPoint** and **Handout** best practice	**LOW** if done well, **HIGH** if done badly
Show of Hands	Ask for opinion or vote via show of hands	— At the start to get an idea of experience or opinion, or at the end to judge comfort with material — Make sure you refer to the results when you move on	**LOW**
Flipchart	Ask attendees for input and record their thoughts Illustrate your thoughts to draw attendees away from slides (eg deal structure) as you talk it through	See below on flipcharts	**LOW** (if practised and planned)

Questions	Ask the audience questions and seek input	— Make sure you have a good (and correct!) answer in case they don't respond — Don't pick on anyone unless they volunteer, or use the method below in pairs	**LOW** (if practised and planned)
Chat in Pairs or with Neighbour	Avoid the awkwardness of a sea of blank faces when you ask questions (as above)	— Ask attendees to chat to the person next to them and come up with some ideas and then feedback — Tell them you're expecting answers at the end of the allotted time — Keep up the pressure on timings, 'you've got 30 seconds left ... 15 seconds left ... etc'	**LOW**

Name	Details	Example and hints	Risk
Quiz	Start your presentation with a short quiz (perhaps on PowerPoint or on a handout in pairs or groups)	— Make sure you have clear, unambiguous answers that you can explain — Give attendees enough time, but keep them under time pressure — Make it fun and energetic – consider using PowerPoint slides to make it engaging and focus the energy. See below for PowerPoint best practice.	**MEDIUM**
Case Study	Focus your presentation on a case study or short scenario to hone in on the key issues and facts.	— Give it a human dimension and make it relevant (use familiar names and ideas) and give out a full answer at the end — Give attendees time to discuss in groups — Make sure it's not too long — Consider using short two-line scenarios if there is a variety of disparate issues	**MEDIUM**

| Role Play | Get one or a few of your attendees up on their feet, taking part in a role play to bring ideas, concepts and issues to life | — Choose only volunteers
— If no one volunteers, pick someone who has contributed confidently earlier in the session; try approaching them beforehand or in a break to warn them, and express gratitude after the exercise has ended
— Be clear on what you're trying to achieve
— Have a brief beforehand and guidelines for feedback (what your audience is looking for?)
— When giving feedback, start with positives and refer to negatives in a positive manner (ie 'what they did badly' becomes 'that was great — what could they have done even better?' | **MEDIUM** to **HIGH** |

Using flipcharts, whiteboards and interactive tools

They may seem intimidating, but using flipcharts or equivalent tools is easy and makes you look super-relaxed, if you adhere to these golden rules:

- Practise writing on your flipchart/board beforehand. Your writing should be legible, clear and large enough for 90 per cent of your audience to see, read and understand it.

- Try to stand so that you don't have your back to your audience when you write on the flipchart/board, ie stand to the side so that you can maintain eye contact intermittently as you write.

- Think about what your flipchart/board is adding to your presentation. Flipcharts should be used either for capturing answers/discussion points from your audience, or for drawing attention away from PowerPoint and tracking an idea or concept (eg an deal structure or personnel chart). Drawing as you talk feels more spontaneous. Don't use a flipchart/board just for the sake of using it.

- Rehearse writing your flipcharts/boards. Know exactly what is going on your flipchart/board before you've asked for input. Whatever you do, don't rely on your audience for inspiration!

- Check you have a pen that doesn't make an irritating noise when you write, or that runs out of ink mid-sentence.

- Take your time when writing. Remember — you're in charge. Don't rush! Record things accurately so that your audience members don't have to pipe up and correct you.

- Use different colours when you get more experienced, to show different ideas and concepts.

- Avoid using SHOUTING capitals and basic grammatical errors (notably, erroneous apostrophes and spelling mistakes).

Lastly and most importantly:

- Make sure you refer to or use information you procure from your audience. Don't just ask, record and then move on without reference. Always have a reason for using a flipchart/board; it shouldn't feel gratuitous.

- Put a title at the top of every flipchart/board page so that your audience will know what you're doing at every stage — it's a joint exercise, not a show.

A simple rule: if someone were to walk in mid-way through your presentation and see you writing on a flipchart, they should be able to tell roughly what your session is about and what you've asked or your audience has provided in terms of contribution, just by looking at the title and the captured points.

Always remember the following when you are interacting in the main body of your presentation:

- Make sure you tie everything back to your objectives and, more importantly, your outcomes to prove that you have covered what you said you intended to cover, and also to prevent your structure from meandering.

- Keep the energy up. When doing group work, if you feel that an interactive portion of your presentation is dragging, it will feel 10-times worse for the attendees. When you hear people discussing the 'X-Factor' and/or 'Eastenders', take back the initiative and carry on.

If you start interacting, don't stop. Invariably, once you have broken the ice, your audience will contribute more and more. Show you are enjoying the interaction and (time permitting) continue asking for input as you go long. Equally, remember that it is always best to plan what you do and do what you plan. You are a lawyer, not an improviser; improvisation will only end in tears.

7. HANDLING CHALLENGING QUESTIONS IN LEGAL PRESENTATIONS?

Table 6.2 below sets out some strategies for dealing with any challenging questions that may crop up during your presentation.

Table 6.2   *Strategies for dealing with challenging questions*

Type of question	Strategy for Dealing
The Interrogator, eg *'What are you talking about? Do you even know what you're saying?'*	Restate your point and specify its source. Maybe ask for elaboration and invite input from the group, or simply ask to discuss at the end, citing time constraints as a reason
The Buffoon, eg *'I'm sorry, I really don't understand that at all, can you explain further?'*	Check with rest of group. If the questioner is alone in not understanding, ask to discuss at the end, citing time constraints as a reason. Or suggest that it was indeed a complicated point and quickly summarise again (deferring until the end if the individual still claims not to have understood)
The Contradictor, eg *'I think you'll find that's incorrect, it's actually …'*	Ask for clarification and source. Explain your reasoning and defer until another time. Do not argue

The Red Herring, eg *'Your story reminds me of a time [unrelated blah, blah …]'*	Depending on timing and seniority, let it run its course. Interject at a clear break in speech and explain time constraints. Ask to hear more afterwards
The Egoist, eg *'I have a lot of experience in that area and I would disagree …'*	Thank for input and ask for elaboration if relevant. Put to group and then take feedback on flipchart, or defer, citing time constraints as the reason

Generally …

There is nothing wrong with not knowing the answer to a tricky question, as long as it isn't something for which you should have prepared. The key is how you deal with the situation.

Do: *thank everyone for their input, no matter how contradictory or wrong; be courteous but firm, citing time constraints as a reason not to dwell; take time to think before answering any questions.*

Don't: *lie or make it up; waffle without thinking; speak without considering your answer; get angry and visibly frustrated; make the person feel stupid or personally attacked; let it put you off course.*

8. USING CRIB-NOTES

If you must ...

Be as economical as you can with paper. **Remember, paper is noisy!** If you're going to use those awful cue-cards, don't have a pack of 200. The more you use, the higher the probability that you'll drop them on the floor and/or lose your way – disaster!

Remember not to use notes for your opener – the opener is learnt, 100 per cent verbatim.

Keep all notes simple. Do what you did at school when you were revising — reduce all prompts to one word or short phrases, and prepare fully so you are 150 per cent familiar with everything in your presentation. Notes are an aid, not a crutch.

Don't speak when you are looking at your notes. Shut up and stay silent when looking down. Open your mouth only when you've collected your thoughts together and are ready to speak articulately, not before!

9. HUMOUR AND THE FUNNIES ...

Humour is a tricky one. Why? Because, generally , people who think they're 'funny' are not funny at all. Lawyers aren't known or recruited for their sense of humour.

However, humour is becoming an increasingly important asset in terms of communication skills at work in law firms. After all, 'funny' sells books, films and plays. Equally, appropriately funny people are valued at work in the law and in business (as long as they back their humour up with intellectual nous).

What senior lawyers and business people find amusing might be very different from what you and your mates find hilarious over a pint of Guinness in the local.

Stick to these rules when delivering presentations at work:

- **Jokes are not your friend**. Jokes have set-ups and punch-lines; they may be funny in the pub, but they will not generally work in an office environment. Never start or end a presentation with a joke. There is a 99 per cent chance that someone important won't find it funny, even if those your age might. Credibility gone.

- **If you must (try to) be funny, make it a funny, true anecdote**. Break the ice with something others can relate to. By all means embellish your anecdote but don't lie and/or exaggerate purely for comedy's sake. Someone will find you out.

- **If you say something you intended to be lightly amusing and it gets no response whatsoever, don't refer to it at all**. Move on **quickly** to something with more substance/gravitas. You're not a comedian, no one is paying you to be funny so there's no need to make excuses. There's nothing more awkward than humour-based self-deprecation, ('Well, I found it funny … that's obviously just my terrible sense of humour'). Awful, truly awful.

10. POWERPOINT AND POWERPOINTERS

PowerPoint has become the curse of the legal professional presenter. It is ritually abused and overused, and has become more of a crutch than an incisive learning aid.

There is nothing wrong in principle with using a slide presentation as long as you can answer the following question in the negative: if I were to arrive in the room and discover that the laptop and projector were both broken, would I panic? If the answer is yes, you are too reliant on your slides and you are a PowerPoint abuser! Shame on you.

To make an impact as a presenter, you need to differentiate yourself by taking the steps suggested in Table 6.3 below.

Table 6.3   *Steps to make you stand out as a presenter*

Stage	Step
Before writing your slideshow	Do everything else! **Creating a PowerPoint presentation should be the last thing you do** before methodically rehearsing your presentation.
Before writing your slideshow	Ask yourself, **do I need PowerPoint presentation**, or could I put this into a handout as a takeaway? If the latter, see below for **Handout Tips**.
Before writing your slideshow	**Write a short bullet-point list of all the main issues** or sub-topics in your presentation **that might require a slide** to create a **PowerPoint Map** (ie a maximum number of slides for your presentation). Be ruthless. When considering whether a point merits a slide, if you are unsure, it doesn't.
Before writing your slideshow	Remember, **if it doesn't add it subtracts**. The more slides, the worse — not the better! Spending hours creating a slideshow with 150 slides is full-on PowerPoint abuse and it is an arrestable offence! **PowerPoint slides are not there to help you remember your presentation.** Stick to your **PowerPoint Map** and don't be tempted to add in slides to remind you of information you are worried you might forget.
While writing your slideshow	**Put all your speaker notes in the 'notes' section** at the bottom of each slide in your editing window. Try to have one document that you revise and from which you rehearse for the whole presentation to avoid confusion. No one minds you having a print-out of your slides in front of you, as long as you don't seem reliant upon them.

When writing your slideshow	**Never include more than six small points or two big points on one slide.**
	Never try to cover an entire, substantive point in full on a slide. Use trigger words and then explain. If the viewers need to remember it, put it in a handout.
When writing your slideshow	**Use the same font and font size all the way through** (in the same colour scheme). Spare a thought for the colour-blind and test your font colour on your chosen background before your presentation. Can you read it from the back of the room?
	With this in mind, **stay away from busy, bright colours on slides.** Be conservative. Very conservative. If you want to show off your personality, use the spoken and not the written word.
When writing your slideshow	**Animate your slides so that there is an element of surprise as they sequence onto the screen.** But do not over-animate or use sound effects. Be tasteful. 'Whoosh' and 'whizz' noises are not appropriate at work.
	Don't make anything 'fly' or 'spiral' into your slide ... ever. Only use the 'blinds' or 'box' methods in the 'entrance' facet of the Custom Animation Function (on the top menu).
When writing your slideshow	**Think of a visual theme** (eg a neat, low-profile image that appears on every slide discreetly in one corner for continuity) **and stick to it.**
	Make sure you check with your internal communications people that your imagery is appropriate and on-brand!

Stage	Step
When writing your slideshow	Just as with humour, **be careful using unrelated 'wacky' imagery designed specifically to get a laugh.** Your audience might have a little chuckle, but it won't send the same subliminal message of authority and credibility to them that a professionally amusing anecdote and an appropriately related image will.
When writing your slideshow	**Check and double-check for typos.** If there's one thing that will make you feel stupid, it's having a small grammatical error blown up on a big screen behind you whilst you're trying to make a lasting, positive impact.
When writing your slideshow	**Don't use photos if you can help it.** They always look terrible, and most people can't see them properly unless they're huge (which looks clumsy and unsubtle).
Before your presentation	**Book a private room, a laptop and a projector, then run through** your presentation with one of your mates over lunch and ask for very specific feedback. Treat this as formally as you can.
Before your presentation	Order a **remote mouse** if possible, to allow you to walk around a bit as you present so that you aren't rigidly tied to a laptop. Don't plan to stand behind a speaker's lectern.
Before your presentation	**Try to arrive in the room at least 10 minutes before your presentation starts**, to have a go with the equipment and set up the room as you'd like it.

At the start of your presentation	**Don't do what all lawyers do and give F slides as a handout**, printed three to a p for notes on the right.
	The first thing your attendees will do is to look for the last slide so that they can switch off. It is also most demoralising for an audience to be given 50 slides in a handout and for the speaker to have covered only two, with 10 minutes to go until the scheduled end!
	Give the attendees the slides as a handout at the end, or circulate by e-mail. If they need to make notes during the presentation, **give them a handout (see below)**. Alternatively, they can make notes in their own note-pads. They should have brought them!
During your presentation	**Don't look behind you at your slides as you talk**, you lose valuable eye contact and it constitutes a clear message to your audience that you are extremely nervous or uncomfortable. Look at the screen in front of you on a laptop or monitor, or at your printed-out slides on a desk in front of you.
During your presentation	**If you decide to spend some time on a topic, black out the slide (press 'B' on the keyboard)** to allow the audience to focus on you and not your PowerPoint show. Press 'B' again to return to the slideshow.
During your presentation	**Never, ever read out lists from a slide – it is patronising and frustrating for your audience.** They can read. Rather, say 'I'll let you read that for a moment' and then summarise the key points briefly without repeating anything verbatim from the slides.
At the end of your presentation	**Have a discrete slide that contains the words 'Thank you'.** It shows you value the audience's time, and again communicates subliminal authority and assertiveness.

11. FANCY USING A HANDOUT?

There is nothing wrong with using appropriately created and numbered PowerPoint slides to help structure your presentation for your audience. Remember, however, that PowerPoint is designed to help your **audience**, and **not to help you** remember the presentation. You should know your material inside-out, slides or no slides. Fail to prepare and prepare to fail!

With your preparation as a given, what about going leftfield and doing the following:

a) reducing the size of your PowerPoint presentation;

b) not giving a print-out of your slides to the audience at the start of your session;

c) creating a separate handout to help your audience make meaningful notes and keep up;

d) giving out your slides only at the end as a wrap-up exercise.

Sound radical? It's guaranteed to make a positive impact — 100 per cent. Why? Because no one remembers a presenter because of his/her slides. Everyone produces slides! Slides invariably go in a file somewhere above a desk, never to be seen or read again.

- Less information on slides means more audience engagement with you. Who really wants to stare at a computer screen for 40 minutes? They can do that at their desks.

- Giving them a nice-looking handout and a reason for them to stick it on the wall in their office will serve as a constant reminder of that excellent presentation they attended that was delivered by that excellent professional — you!

- It's more environmentally-friendly!

If you take the plunge and decide to produce a handout, follow these five simple rules:

1. Make it easy to follow and congruent with your presentation.

2. In your introduction, explain how the audience members might use it so they know they aren't getting slides on which to make notes and expectations are met.

3. Put your name, the date and your presentation title on the handout in bold font, so that it can be clearly associated with you and your material after the presentation. Someone else sees it and word travels ...

4. Brand your handout and take time to make it look attractive. It's an extension of you! Remember learning styles and try to incorporate something visual (eg a flow-chart) to cater for all styles.

5. Stop at regular intervals to allow your audience to take notes. Budget for this when timing your presentation in your run-through.

12. LOOKING GOOD, SOUNDING PROFESSIONAL AND FEELING GREAT

Most lawyers cite nerves as the reason for their under-confidence when presenting. However, nerves are simply your body's natural 'flight or fight' response to perceived stress. In that moment, when the adrenalin surges and your blood vessels widen to maximise oxygen flow to the vital organs, so the theory goes, you will never fight harder or run faster.

It seems logical (if fighting or running isn't appropriate) that, armed with the extra adrenalin, you should present more professionally and with added gusto and edge ... if you have prepared properly. Lack of preparation, coupled with the adrenalin, the extra oxygen and large butterflies in the tummy, is sure to create panic without warning. If presenting makes you nervous, therefore, it's even more important that you negate the effects by preparing rigorously. That way, your nerves will help keep you sharp, fresh and on-the-ball.

Conversely, if you are a really confident presenter, you might not have those nerves to heighten your performance. You will, however, need to prepare just as much (arguably more!). 'Winging it' is bound to back-fire. After all, whilst an audience might feel a little bit sorry for a nervous presenter who hasn't prepared properly, no one is going to spare any sympathy for the cocky presenter who hasn't bothered to spend time getting his head straight before launching into a 40-minute lecture debacle.

What about the visual elements, though? How can those nerves affect your visual performance or brand? After all, no matter how much we prepare, sometimes nerves just get the better of us. Even if that is the case, we still need to communicate a sense of outward calmness to our audience to prevent them from losing confidence in our ability to keep them engaged.

Table 6.4 below suggests some methods to suggest this state of calm professionalism.

Table 6.4 *How to achieve 'calm, charming professional' when presenting*

Be philosophical	You are at work and not in a comedy club doing an open spot. The chances are your audience will be on your side and will not heckle. They're listening because they think you have something useful say. Remain optimistic.
The start	If your audience members are chatting amongst themselves and you need to get going, rather than quietly beginning without their full attention, show them you mean to start. Move to your starting position, stand or sit completely still, and smile at and engage eye contact with at least three people in your audience who will spread the word that you are intending to start. Then wait until it is almost quiet so everyone can hear, and begin. Repeat your first words calmly if there is a noise.

Learn your start verbatim, especially your opener and introduction. Smile before speaking to show you are happy to be there. |

Smile	Smile regularly throughout your presentation. You would be amazed how serious and earnest most lawyers look when they present. Remember, people buy people. People smile.
Speech	Be deliberate in pronouncing every word, especially those lazy consonants. Don't use any slang or become too conversational at the start of your talk. Moderate this throughout.
Pace	Practise your full presentation in front of a friend (see below for some ideas) and go slowly enough that it feels slightly uncomfortable for you when you hear yourself. It won't feel uncomfortable for your audience at all, just calm and measured. You can never speak too slowly; just ask Barack Obama! Adhere to the two/three-second rule when speaking — pause for two seconds at the end of every sentence and for three seconds at the end of every paragraph or idea. This is very important.
Ummm ...	Don't worry about umming. When you have your rehearsal with a friend, ask him to tell you if you over-ummm. Even if you do, it's not fatal if you have a clear and communicable structure. Just being aware of your tendency to ummm will stop you doing it as much. The bottom line: focus on being 100 per cent comfortable with your subject-matter and ummming will seem a distant memory. Ummm...
Eyes	Do not stare at that one person you know or that one awkward person who seems disengaged. Spread the love and show you are engaging with everyone as people. Whatever you do, don't retreat into your notes. Eye contact is a key rapport-building tool. Miss out on doing it and your audience will think you don't care.

Sit or stand?	If standing, be as still as possible when you are making a serious point or summarising a key issue. If sitting, lean in, never cross your legs and make an even more deliberate effort with eye-contact.
Legs and feet	Moving around is fine, subject to the above; shifting and rocking is not. It says 'mental' or 'criminal' and not 'professional'. When you are standing, stand deliberately still.
Hands	Gesticulating is absolutely fine — but not at the start, when you make important points or at the end when you are summing up. At these times, it is vital that the audience looks at your face and are not distracted by the visual 'noise' produced by your hands and arms.
	Generally, hands should not be in pockets but should rather be held together or loosely clasped (subject to gesticulation) around your lower abdomen (not your groin).
Props	There is nothing wrong with holding something to occupy your hands if you feel awkward. Just don't play with the prop (eg clicking a pen-lid or a ball-point button).
Water	Never present without water. No one wants to listen to your gummy, dry mouth when you speak. Sip regularly and when you are finishing a point, topic or issue, to show finality and that you are ready to move on. This actually looks very composed and learned. Take your time when you sip. Water dribbling down the chin isn't a good look for a lawyer.

Watch	Take off your watch and place it on the desk in front of you. It allows you to keep a track of time and shows your audience that you care about how long you're going to be speaking so they can get back to their desks in time for that conference-call.
Dress	This is simple; be as formal as the most formal person in the room. This means assume suit and tie (equivalent for women) as a default before you get to the room.
Shut up	If you lose your place, there is nothing wrong with taking time to consolidate and find your bearings. If you decide to look down at some notes, shut your mouth and don't speak. The two activities do not go together. If you talk into notes, you lose the projection you might achieve if you were to speak forward and out. You also lose eye contact.
Be yourself	Don't try to be something or someone you're not. Presenting might not be your strongest suit. That's not to say you can't become highly competent without being a genius. Follow the above, prepare properly, and you'll meet and exceed all expectations! That's a promise!

Useful questions to ask a colleague after completing a dry-run of your presentation

Always try to have a dry-run of your presentation with a trusted friend or colleague. The more important the presentation, the more important the rehearsal. Don't assume that the shorter the slot, the less rehearsal you need. Often, the hardest presentations are those that have to be shoehorned into a tiny time-slot. After completing your rehearsal, consider asking your observer some or all of the following questions:

- Can you tell me what you think my overall message was?

- Were my objectives and outcomes clearly communicated to you at the start?

- What knowledge have you gained from my presentation?

- What practical help have you gained from my presentation?

- Was my structure clear all the way through?

- Was the balance between theory and advice ok?

- Did I seem to have an opinion on the subject, or did I come across as a legal-technical drone?

- Did I seem relaxed when I interacted with you?

- Did I seem comfortable with the flipchart (if appropriate)?

- Did I seem reliant on my slides (if appropriate)?

- Was my presentation, out of 10, highly stressful or highly enjoyable?

- Did I seem to be enjoying myself? If not, why?

13. DEMYSTIFYING LEGAL PRESENTATION SKILLS – SUMMARY

- Be yourself and be philosophical; you're a lawyer (not an actor or a wacky advertising executive) delivering a presentation at work (not in a comedy club), and no one is expecting you to perform like a politician or a comic.

- Plan and prepare using our structure model, and don't worry yourself with the performance aspects until you are 100 per cent comfortable with your subject-matter. Then have a run-through with a trusted colleague and ask for feedback on all elements of your presentation.

- Remember, your opener is about YOU; your introduction is about YOUR PRESENTATION. Forget this and you miss a really important scene-setting and personal-branding opportunity.

- Be completely still for the first two minutes of your presentation.

- Remember to smile when you begin and intermittently throughout.

- Speak more slowly than feels comfortable.

- Sip water regularly to combat 'dry-mouth syndrome'.

- Use a separate handout instead of PowerPoint slides in handout form.

- Never give out PowerPoint slides at the start of your presentation; if you have to, circulate them by e-mail afterwards.

- Be honest when answering questions; you can afford to at your level!

- Enjoy it — the adrenalin rush associated with an important and successful presentation is like no other feeling in business!

7

Be Grammatical – Fewer Errors Means Greater Impact

INTRODUCTION

For the twenty-first-century solicitor, talking — and even walking — with flair and panache are not enough to make the distinction between being run-of-the-mill and being exceptional. In this age of instant communication, of hasty e-mails and dashed-off letters that, thanks to word processers, look plausible but make poor sense, clear and grammatically-sound writing is a basic tool for success. Basic, but often fraught with possible pitfalls.

We're not talking about legal drafting. This book is not designed to help you 'do' the law. You'll learn legal drafting skills from those around you. We're talking about basic grammatical mistakes in documents, which dramatically reduce your chances of getting the opportunity to draft anything vaguely technical. No one will trust you to do that. And if you keep on making those mistakes as a junior, no one will want to work with you as you become more and more senior. Your career will end up in a professional cul-de-sac.

The truth is, as bright young things, you probably think writing is a doddle. You got good grades at school, your university essays got you a First Class degree and you might have achieved a Distinction in your LPC. Writing is your bread and butter, you think. That is, until, before you know it, a shifty apostrophe or an underhand gerund (did you even know there were such things?) throws you right off course. Instead of coming across as articulate and wise, you're perceived as an idiot.

The best writing is not noticed, but while the experienced lawyers you work with may not shake you by the hand for not overusing commas, your unrelenting excellence in this regard will contribute subliminally to a very positive, professional, internal personal brand. Bad writing, on the other hand, is more glaring than the proverbial sore thumb. External clients, paying your firm £400 per hour, will justifiably wonder what hope there is for accurate legal advice when you can't even spell.

Vigilance is called for. The vigilance must be yours, but, to flag up the dangers that lie in wait, we set out below the 'Ten Most Wanted' of good writing — the rogues to look out for as you put together letters to make words, words to make sentences, sentences to make paragraphs, and paragraphs to make … well, letters, memos, notes and e-mails.

Table 7.1   *The 'Naming of Parts'*

THE NAMING OF PARTS – some of the things we never learnt at primary school, were taught but didn't take in or, if we did, may have long forgotten.
Take a look at the following sentence, hold your hand over the information below, and try to remember the name and function of each word: **The sun slowly emerged and it turned into a beautiful day.** **The** — definite article; one of those little words, like 'a' or 'an', that precede and modify nouns; **sun** — a noun; this applies to people, places and things. **slowly** — an adverb; generally ending in '-ly', adverbs tell us more about verbs.

emerged — a verb; past tense, conveying the action in a sentence; a 'doing' word.

and — a conjunction; a joining word — links the clauses of the sentence, showing their relationship to one another.

it — a pronoun; used in place of a noun for clarity and concision.

turned — another verb, past tense.

into — a preposition; it describes the relationship between two words, in this case 'turn' and 'day'.

a — another article, this time an indefinite one.

beautiful — an adjective; it describes another person or thing.

day — another noun.

Table 7.2   *Class distinction*

Did you know that class distinction is not confined to the human world? The English language also has its divisions, based not so much on variety but on stability and longevity.

OPEN CLASSES include words that constantly change and evolve, making the English language a living, breathing organism. They include nouns ('Internet', 'cinema'), verbs ('to text') adjectives (eg 'technological') and adverbs (eg electronically).

CLOSED CLASSES of words are fixed and unchanging, keeping our language a stable and reliable means of communication. These are the small but vital conjunctions, pronouns, prepositions and articles.

THE 'TEN MOST WANTED' OF GOOD WRITING

Here goes:

1. My, my, what a very long sentence you have!

And what amazing adjectives and conjunctions and verbal control. But how convoluted and unnecessarily complicated, and — gosh — almost too many words to comprehend. The message here is that there is no merit in a long sentence if it interferes with the clarity of your message. Keep it simple. Keep it coherent. Your reader should notice the brilliance of your deductions and the depth of your knowledge rather than the density of your prose. A successful sentence should have to be read only once to make perfect sense. And be wary of over-using commas. Remember that commas, as well as having a grammatical role to play in sentences, also indicate where to take a breath when reading aloud. If you get breathless, perhaps a few full-stops are called for!

2. Keep active when you can

In life, as in writing, the opposite of being active is being passive – and no one wants to be that. Certain lawyers have a tendency to favour the passive in the mistaken belief that it comes across as more intellectual. This is the wrong approach.

Take a look at an active sentence: *'Ted loves Mary.'* In its passive form it would read as follows: *'Mary is loved by Ted.'* It is the same situation, but told back to front using 40 per cent more words. So — apart from reducing wordiness, a merit in itself — why is the active voice preferred to the passive in written communication?

The passive voice can be awkward; it can also be vague and come across as perhaps a little devious. That is possibly why politicians and utility companies tend to favour it. For example: 'Bombs were dropped' and 'Shots were fired' and 'Your electricity is to be disconnected.' Notice that the passive voice masks responsibility for the bombs, the shots and the power cut. Active voice, on the other hand, implies that the writer is concise and straightforward, which is exactly how you, as twenty-first-century Solicitor, want to be perceived. So, when possible, stay active.

3. To split or not to split?

We are talking about infinitives here (eg 'to fight'). The offence of tearing them apart in a sentence would, in the old days, have been severely punished. For someone to have written 'to bravely fight' instead of 'to fight bravely' (thus splitting the full infinitive with an adverb) was seen as a grave crime against the English language. Common usage, however, has mellowed – infinitives are split with impugnity in everyday speech. So is it acceptable, then, to go on a wild spree and rip infinitives asunder with abandon? Perhaps not. There are some cranky pseudo-pedants who believe it their duty to slap the wrists of any infinitive splitter, so why do it when, wrongly or not, it might offend? Your supervisor, for instance, could pride himself on being a stickler for 'correct' grammar, so why make his hackles rise by writing, say, 'to legally challenge' when 'to challenge legally' would do as well?

4. Beware, my friend, of the dangling participle

This is a syntactical hazard that can bring about confusion or misinformation, or – far, far worse — can transform you instantly from rising star into laughing stock. Not good.

Syntactical? That needs some explaining before we get to grips with the 'dangle'. It's the adjectival form of the term syntax, meaning sentence structure, which (you may recall from the classroom) involves not only subjects and objects and verbs, but also things like clauses and phrases. So, for example, we begin with this simple sentence:

My <u>supervisor</u> (*subject*) <u>fixed</u> (*verb*) the <u>computer monitor</u> (*object*)

Then we add an adjectival <u>clause</u> — which means a group of words <u>containing a verb</u> — which tells us more about a noun in your sentence.

Thus:

> **My supervisor, who <u>fancies himself as an IT expert,</u> (*adjectival clause*) fixed the computer monitor.**

Then, to embellish our sentence further, we add an adjectival phrase — which means a group of words <u>without a verb</u>. Thus:

> **My supervisor, who fancies himself as an IT expert, fixed <u>that near-obsolete</u> (*adjectival phrase*) computer monitor.**

Brilliant. Our sentence is sprouting wings. However, we decide on a little judicial editing, thus:

> **Having broken down again, my supervisor, who fancies himself as an IT expert, fixed that near-obsolete ...**

Hold it there! What's happening? Instead of telling us about the condition of the computer monitor, the adjectival clause seems to make allusion to the supervisor's state of mind. A case of mistaken modification. A potentially embarrassing instance of the dreaded dangling participle. Get it?

Here is another example, to make the point clear:

> **Reaching home, the sun came out.**

Again, *oops*. Who reached home, the author or the sun? The dangling participle can be sneakily subversive, so be alert. If in doubt, read your work through again. And again. Aloud, if possible — bearing in mind that unaccompanied mumbling in a small, shared office can compromise your professional dignity.

5. Avoiding ambiguity with hope

This is something we should always do or, at least, aspire to as we make our wary path up the legal ladder. As Robert Louis Stephenson famously wrote, 'To travel hopefully is a better thing than to arrive.' The catch here is the word 'hopefully', which we tend to use without due care.

Stephenson, we imagine, intended his sentence to imply that it is better to travel filled with hope than to reach one's destination. Our current use of the word might offer the following interpretation: 'To travel is, I hope, better than to arrive.' A subtle — or perhaps less-than-subtle — difference, but indicative of how the usage of the word has changed.

Does it matter, though?

Hopefully not.

Meaning, *I hope it does not.*

But pedants can take offence at the liberal employment of the word, not to mention its close cousins 'apparently', 'presumably', 'mercifully', 'thankfully' and the rest. Take the sentence, 'Hopefully, the rain will soon stop.' Here, the H-word can suggest that it is the rain being hopeful and not the author. After all, we would hardly say, 'Believably, the rain will soon stop,' if we believed it might, or 'Thinkingly, the rain will soon stop,' if we thought it would.

Using 'hopefully' is hardly a hanging (or dangling) offence, but may be regarded with suspicion for the following two reasons:

- It can cause ambiguity. For example, in the following sentence, 'We will go to the meeting, hopefully, straight after lunch,' it is not clear whether 'hopefully' refers to the author's state of mind or to the time the meeting is scheduled to take place.

- It is a weak word. Unspecific. 'Hopefully, the Underground workers' strike will end today.' Who is hoping? The writer? The workers? All right-minded people? Like the use of the passive voice (see above), the word can be an easy way to evade responsibility for an action or opinion. Hopefully, therefore, you'll avoid it.

Creative lawyers?! Hang on ...

So you think being a lawyer means suppressing your creative side? That, as a knowledgeable and respected professional, your writing has above all to be succinct and authoritative — and that 'succinct and authoritative' automatically means 'dry and dull'? Wrong. You need to be concise, certainly, for no one has time for long-winded verbosity. And authoritative — *definitely*. You know your stuff and your writing should reflect this.

But dry and dull? Never. If you know exactly what you want to say and to whom you are saying it; if your piece of writing follows a logical progression that stems from your familiarity with the subject and the lucidity of your mind, then it will generate its own energy. And with that kind of purposeful energy, not even the most technical document need be dry or dull.

Now clearly (as a novelist) I cannot comment on either your level of knowledge or your lucidity. For the first you have professional guidance and for the second I recommend good sleeping habits and a healthy diet. But I can, in a general sense, talk about the principles of good business writing, of which imagination is as important a component as familiarity with verbs and nouns. And you — with the intellect and powers of deduction which you, as lawyers, are almost certainly endowed —can particularise these principles to your ends.

What do I mean, though, about 'imagination' ... 'creativity'? Surely these are the indulgences of artistes and degenerates with nothing on their mind but to hang about, drunk usually, awaiting inspiration? Clearly they have nothing in common with the up-and-coming solicitor that is you?

But perhaps you'd sit up and attend more closely if I were to tell you, however, that these nebulous-seeming tools can:

- impress your colleagues, superiors and clients with your astuteness and insight, and;

- guard against giving offence (or worse) by using inappropriate language, form or mode of address.

'Creativity' is the third of what I call the Textual Trinity — the three pillars of good writing, business or otherwise. The first two are Clarity and Coherence.

Clarity and Coherence refer to clear, logical thinking and practical application. Is your piece of writing a request for information? Is its purpose to convey information? An apology? An instruction? If you understand the aim of your document and the reasoning behind it, it can help you to plan the most logical sequence in which to present your material. Providing, of course, you're adept at the nuts and bolts of writing, the basic tools of language such as grammar, spelling and punctuation. To this end, style and grammar guides abound — with some of the most glaring stumbling blocks listed on these pages.

Which brings us back to Creativity. This is the ingredient that can intangibly lift your writing from the workmanlike to the influential. If Clarity and Coherence are the 'how' and 'what' of good written communication, then Creativity is the 'who'. And since writing is about people — it has to be; in its various forms it the most advanced means of communication we have — understanding the 'who' of your document is crucial. There are two aspects to consider:

- Who are you writing to?
- Who are you writing as?

The first is obvious. If you are addressing a letter to a client, try and imagine him or her, much as a novelist would imagine a character in fiction. Consider his/her level of understanding, state of mind, age perhaps. There is no need to patronise or kowtow — simply have your audience in mind as you write and adjust the tone appropriately.

The second aspect you may dismiss as ridiculously self-evident. Don't. Clearly, if it's a work-related document, you are writing as a lawyer. Think on, though. As a respected lawyer, would you, in your professional life, use platitudes or colloquialism or the kind of language that you might privately employ? We all juggle with several roles and sometimes the language appropriate for one (your mate/parent/children) can slip into another. Being clearly aware of the particular voice you're using at a particular time calls for imagination. Particularly when you don't feel like a successful young lawyer but you have to write like one.

Shelley Weiner

(Journalist, Novelist, Creative Writing Lecturer and Mentor and Royal Literary Fund Fellow)

www.shelleyweiner.com

6. Faulty apostrophe = image catastrophe

Did you know that those innocuous-seeming little marks that you (sometimes carelessly) sprinkle over your writing have the power to scream to your seniors that you are **Not Partner Material**. They may appear tiny and inoffensive – dots with or without curly tails, bland dashes, harmless hyphens. But don't be fooled. Like the Nanovirus, the ill-placed punctuation mark has toxic potential that far exceeds its size. And the one to fear especially, the Anthrax of the punctuation arsenal, is that enemy of all upward mobility, the apostrophe.

Used correctly, the apostrophe has two main functions:

- **To show possession**. As in 'the girl's hat', 'the man's briefcase', 'the woman's handbag', 'everyone's duty', 'no one's responsibility'.

  BUT ...

  Personal pronouns (words like I, you, he, she, it, we, they) indicate the possessive by becoming a whole new word. These new words are already possessive, so they don't need an apostrophe: my, mine, your, yours, his, her, hers, its, our, ours, their, theirs. Note that **none of them has an apostrophe**.

- **To show that some letters have been omitted in a word or words**, ie to indicate a contraction. As in *don't*, and *isn't*, and *you're* here, and *I'm* there.

  BUT ...

  There are exceptions, as in *CD*, not *C'D'*; *photo*, not *photo'*. And note especially that **where you wouldn't use an apostrophe in the singular, do not use it for the plural**. Thus: I bought four CDs (**NOT CD's**); we took several photos (**NOT photo's**).

Knowing **when** to use the apostrophe is one thing, **where** to place it is another.

In general, it goes **directly after the thing doing the possessing**. Get it?

Look at some examples: 'The Queen's palace' (the palace of the Queen); 'My mother's photos' (photos belonging to my mother); 'one month's notice' (notice of one month); three years' experience (experience of three years ... note that when a word is plural, the apostrophe generally comes after the 's').

Having mastered the when and where of the apostrophe, there's the if to consider — that is, when NOT to use the apostrophe at all. The answer is, when there is no possessive connection. For example, the dog's bone = the bone belonging to the dog – no confusion there. But 'sports car' describes the car rather than indicates possession. As does 'accounts department'.

7. Don't be ambushed by the slippery ITS/IT'S twins

Although this is technically an apostrophe issue, the twins have such power to induce error and humiliation that they deserve a heading to themselves. Your defence is quite simple. Just two points to remember:

- When *its* is used in its possessive form ('The cat hurt its paw') it **never** takes an apostrophe.

- When *it's* is used as a contraction for *it is*, this is **the only time** it takes an apostrophe.

Remember this. There are few things more irritating for the reader and demeaning to the writer than the ill-punctuated 'its' — and few things easier to get right.

8. The purpose of the semi-colon: clarity or obfuscation?

Semi-colons, it seems, are the mixed spice and smoked paprika of the punctuation world – randomly produced from the back of the store cupboard to ring the changes from dull full-stops and boring commas. Why? Does anyone know?

'Well ... um ... ,' you answer. 'Isn't it because the semi-colon signifies a pause longer than a comma and shorter than a full-stop?'

Partly correct. That is what it indicates. But the real question is: '*When* *should it be used?'* Only in two grammatical situations:

- As a replacement for 'and' in two clauses that have the capacity to stand alone, eg I went to the supermarket; I saw it was closed for the holidays.

- When making a list, as in: 'She met three men: James, who came from New York; Jeremy, the butcher's son; and George, who was very good looking.'

Fortunately you don't have to choose between James, Jeremy and George. You don't have to produce the semi-colon either, unless you are *sure* you're using it correctly. Our advice is to keep it tucked away with the mixed spice unless you are certain your recipe calls for it.

9. Spelling snares that lie in wait to trip you up

Despite our reliance on the spell-checking facility of our word-processing program – or maybe because of it — we still tend to be stymied by some, or all, of the following (you're welcome to add your personal bugbears to the list):

- Accommodate

- Acknowledgement (the American spelling is acknowledgment).

- Commitment

- Consensus

- Deductible

- Dependent (as an adjective in British English; the noun would be '*a dependant*'. Tricky – your spell-checker doesn't know this!)

- Disc**reet** (as in sensitive) or disc**rete** (as in on its own)

- Embarrass

- Existence
- Foreword (as in the preface to a book – but forward to indicate movement. Again, your spell-checker is unaware.)
- Harass
- Inadvertent
- Indispensable
- Judgment (referring to a judicial decision — in American English it's *judgement*.)
- Liaison
- License (as a verb — *to license your vehicle*; as a noun it's licence — *my driving licence*. The US spelling is, confusingly, the other way round)
- Occasion
- Occurrence
- Perseverance
- Practise (as with license/licence, the verb takes an s and the noun takes a c — *He practises as a solicitor; I must get on with my piano practice*. Again note that the US do it vice versa!)
- Prerogative
- Privilege
- Separate
- Supersede
- Withhold

10. Don't be caught napping on the e-mail watch

It's very tempting to relax when composing or replying to an e-mail – tempting but extremely dangerous. We all know of cases of **Ill-advised Forwarding of Unsuitable Material to Superiors and Others**. We have laughed (a little uncomfortably) when a colleague succumbs to **Random Pressing of the Send Button**, thus delivering to a boss's inbox a message intended for a friend or partner — containing unflattering allusions to said boss — causing embarrassment (at best) or dismissal (at worst). And so on, and so on.

So the rule here is: **Think before you press!**

Other pointers regarding the judicious use of e-mail for business:

- Remember it is e-mail *for business*, so do not abandon the formalities that apply to other written communication. 'Hi' is not acceptable (but see below). Neither is 'love', 'cheers', or those ubiquitous xxxxs.

- Stay aloof from the circulation of jokes and the forwarding of (non-work) group e-mails. You'll probably be seen as the office killjoy, but at least you'll retain your dignity.

- Structure your e-mail as though it were a letter — introduction, main body and proper salutation, as in 'Dear', 'Kind regards', 'Many thanks', etc. The tone may be slightly less formal than a letter, but straying on the side of formality is safer than coming across as slack. Stay away from 'Best' as a sign-off and use 'Hi' only when other more senior colleagues have done the same with e-mails to that contact. And **never** use 'Txt Spk' — type out each word, however pressed for time you are.

- If you have a history of pressing 'Reply' without consideration – or, worse, 'Reply All' — then shun these buttons altogether in favour of using 'Forward' and then typing in the appropriate address(es). Safety is paramount.

- Print out important e-mails and spell-check them by scrolling a ruler over each line in hard-copy form and not on-screen.

SUMMARY

This is only a brief introductory guide to good writing. It is not intended to be patronising. It is simply a summary of the key mistakes made and hot-spots identified in business, not just in law firms.

An important consideration is that sometimes you will spot an error in someone else's writing, or see something erroneously corrected in yours. In this situation, decide which fires are best to fight and which to leave in the hope that they will burn themselves out. There might be stylistic issues involved, and while you might want to raise a potential issue, you should consider doing what your influential supervisor tells you to do (even if you think it might be technically incorrect) just to preserve sensitive egos. Our rules are the English language rules. They are correct but you might not see them adopted in your chosen law firm by those you need to impress. The point is, as with communication skills, you might have to adapt your writing style to suit your senior colleagues' style until you have earned the right to impose your own style on others.

8

Be Sociable, Be Likeable and Be Well-Connected

Networking as a junior commercial lawyer

Slip the word 'networking' into a conversation with your average commercial lawyer and they will assume you are talking about an 'event' where a large collection of business people hang about in a room to listen to a boring and/or awkward talk and/or Q&A session delivered by someone underwhelming and uninspiring but quite 'important' (of whom they are supposed to be in awe), followed by a largely inedible buffet and a chance to avoid eye contact with anyone tedious by catching up with e-mails on their Blackberry handset in the corner, finished with a quick exit as soon as it isn't rude to leave (in any event once the free wine has been consumed and/or abandoned). Phew!

It's fair to say that formal networking events, although sometimes unavoidable, are officially horrific 99 per cent of the time, especially where lawyers are involved. Why? It's simple: no one wants to be there.

A number of other factors combine to undermine one's ability to find a connection with someone else at such an event, namely:

- These events are usually held in the evening after a long day, when you would rather be having fun with your mates, your family or your partner.

- There's a good chance you might get stuck chatting to or have to approach someone you would never talk to out of choice.

- If held at a time when everyone would usually be eating, you'll be expected to balance a humiliatingly complex combination of crockery and glassware using only one finger, whilst maintaining articulate, intellectual conversation.

- There is a risk you might suffer the indignity of being ditched yourself – even worse if it is by someone you yourself find catastrophically boring.

Fundamentally, however, no one likes to be told to be friendly. Just as no one likes to be told to smile when they don't feel happy, or to 'chill out' when they feel angry. Similarly, being told to network at a specific place and time is a sure-fire way to guarantee it does not happen.

The good news for you is that, luckily, as a junior commercial lawyer, you won't be attending many formal networking events. Why? Because, frankly, you're probably not deemed to be important enough by those in charge. Things might be slightly different if your firm is very small and junior lawyers are co-responsible for developing business. In medium to large-sized firms, however, if it's a discrete business development and networking event, partners and senior lawyers will generally attend. If it's a marketing event, marketing staff, partners and senior lawyers will generally attend. And on most occasions, they won't ask you to tag along. Sophisticated politics and hierarchy rule this regime. Some would argue that you haven't proved yourself capable of formal networking until you reach a certain level of PQE.

The likelihood is, however, that you are probably pretty good at building rapport, relationships and generating conversation – the essential ingredients of networking. You might be better at it than many of your new senior colleagues. This is where the opportunity lies for you to stand out. By following some simple rules and relying on your natural ability to find common ground, make people like you and to establish social credibility, you can hone your networking skills at the start of your career so that when you eventually do get to attend a formal networking event, you'll cash in whilst others wear the rollerball function out on their Blackberry.

WHAT DOES NETWORKING MEAN FOR YOU?

The reality is that with the advent of online networking (Facebook, Linkedin and even Twitter), formal events are becoming less and less common and less and less important. As such, networking for you means less networking (the verb) and more cultivating a network (the noun). And, surprise surprise, it isn't rocket science. It is what you should be doing everyday; internal and external relationship-building, being calm, light-hearted, likeable, bright and charming. And the key to this, just like being commercial, lies in showing a genuine interest in the people you meet, both in your professional capacity as a lawyer and in your non-professional capacity as a human being. There are no tricks, no formulae, no magic action plan. You have probably been doing it for years without being aware of it. And in many ways, everything we have covered in this book is aimed at helping you to cultivate a network to make the right impact when starting out.

As we know, the best commercial lawyers are likeable, well-connected and command high organisational visibility, both internally and externally. They seem to know or know of everyone. They always seem to have the time to chat (if not now, then later). They listen attentively whenever you talk. They ask questions to show they are listening when relevant, and they react calmly and appropriately to what others say, do or ask. Is seems silly, therefore, for us to pin all of this to one word ('networking'). However, if you were to identify 'objectives' in building a network, they might be as follows:

1. **Stay visible** - maximise your chances of being asked to contribute to an internal presentation, training session or client seminar.

2. **Be supported** - know people whom you trust to help you when you are in a pickle.

3. **Add value** - create links with people internally and externally so that you pop into their heads when they need something from someone at your level.

4. **Have fun** – life is much better when one feels popular.

To achieve these objectives, you might combine the following with everything else you have read in this book:

1. Don't just think legal.

Given that your hours will probably be long whatever you do, why not get involved in some extra-curricular activities? Corporate Social Responsibility (CSR) initiatives are always a good start. You can attend charitable functions and join committees at work, and meet all kinds of people in a non fee-earning or Client Relationship Management (CRM) capacity. It is a great way to up your visibility inside and outside the firm. Be the sender of firm-wide non fee-earning related e-mail. Be the person who gets up at the Christmas party or departmental away-day and announces the charity-raffle winner, or who runs a warm-up game for the team. Show your human side in the local community playground by painting a wall with a senior partner. Establishing common ground in this way is just as effective in building trust as taking a note at a meeting with that partner. Firm-wide, non-work activities allow you establish rapport outside the rigid hierarchichal constraints of the firm. In this way a senior colleague can become less than just a name at the foot of an e-mail and more a genuine contact in the organisation.

Good at sport? Join, administrate or even manage a sports team at work. Try to get yourself playing against clients. Even better if they are short of a player or two. You can join their team and help them win the game against your firm. Clients love that. And you'll have an opportunity to make an impression and some useful contacts at the same time.

2. Fancy some lunch?

If your office has a work canteen, try going down entirely on your own once or twice a week and sitting with some new people you don't know very well. It isn't a crime to ask whether you might join a group of people, as long as you don't sit there and simply stare. It is work, after all, and not a trendy bar in central London! To begin with, stick to junior colleagues. Eventually, they will introduce you to others who are more senior. How the network grows ...

3. Act like an adult and not a moody teenager.

If you find yourself somewhere where you don't know anyone and you need to socialise or chat (eg a conference, a training course, or even another law firm), just relax, act like an adult and be yourself:

- Put your Blackberry away.

- Smile and make eye contact with someone else who is also on his/her own.

- Walk over and introduce yourself, '*Hi, I am [Name]. Where have you come from today?*'

- Once introductions have been made, pick up on something that person has said to ask another question and start a conversation, eg:

- '*Oh, you have come from Manchester. Was it an easy journey this morning?*'

- '*I think I've done some work with your law firm previously, do you know …*'

- '*Do you know much about this course? What are you hoping this course covers?*'

- '*Do you know anyone else here?*'

- '*What does your job involve?*'

- '*Have you attended a course like this before*'?

- '*How have you found today?*'

- '*Do you know much about the speakers?*'

- '*Are you busy at the moment?*'

- *'How are you finding things at the moment? Getting a lot of new work?'*

- *'How long have you been at [FIRM]?'*

You have now started a conversation. Relax into it. Remember, people generally like to talk about themselves. Asking questions is a good way to show you are interested and to build trust and credibility. If you receive monosyllabic responses to your questions, consider whether your questions are too 'closed' (eg 'Have you been here before?', to which the conversation cul-de-sac answer is either 'yes' or 'no'). If so, go with more open questions to begin with (eg 'What kind of work do you do?') to gather information. This should give you material to ask further questions as the conversation develops.

4. Manage the situation assertively.

If you need to move on from a conversation, say the following confidently and with a nice smile and you won't offend anyone:

'It's been really great to meet you, [OPTIONAL: here's my business card], I'm just going to catch up with a few more people but it was great to chat. Let's stay in touch.'

If drinks are available, never offer someone a drink and then disappear without getting one. Never use needing to visit the toilet as an excuse to terminate a conversation – there's a good chance that person will follow you into the toilet if he/she is awkward enough. Never start a conversation with a new person in a lift, on stairs or in an escalator, in a toilet or near a urinal.

5. Follow-up.

Get yourself on LinkedIn and 'link in' with people you come across in a professional (and non-professional) capacity after events and meetings - if appropriate. If someone gives you his/her business card, read it before putting it in your pocket. This sends a subliminal message that you care. Never throw a card away or shove it in a drawer somewhere in your desk never to be looked at again. To be extra-proactive, send your new contact a very short e-mail 24 hours after meeting, re-introducing yourself to cement that person as a contact in your network. This is assertive, high-status and confident behaviour. The wording might be something along the lines:

Dear XXX

I very much enjoyed meeting you at XXX on [DATE].

Here are my contact details. It would be great to catch up for a coffee [some time]/[next time you are in town/nearby]. In the meantime, [INSERT HERE A STATEMENT TO BUILD RAPPORT AND SHOW YOU LISTENED TO THE CONTACT, eg I do hope you managed to get to the station in time to get your train to Manchester!]

Kind regards,

[Your name]

It will also look very impressive to others (more senior than you) if you can recommend someone you met independently by sending them a contact file from Outlook or even make the introduction yourself!

6. Build relationships at the lower levels.

That junior barrister with whom you worked on that case, that junior administrator at the client's organisation to whom you sent some mundane documents, that trainee you worked with on the other side in a transaction - in 10 years' time, these people will be 10 years more senior, just like you. Don't be short-sighted - focus now on contacts who might be junior in their fields like you. Build rapport, solid trust and meaningful credibility, and in 10 years, when you are a partner, they might be a director, a senior partner, executive or even QC! If you have consistently invested in the relationship for a number of years, you might find you have some very influential friends in powerful places.

7. Walk the floors - be physically visible on your floor.

Take time to walk the floors every week, sticking your head round someone's door if they don't look too busy for a quick chat. If they are legal staff, start the conversation with work-related chat to establish how busy they are, and then move on to non work-related chat to build rapport if instigated by them.

Make sure you chat to others (eg that secretarial co-ordinator, events executive or learning and development manager) as you walk around. If your firm is smaller, make a conscious effort to keep in regular contact with your head of HR or HR team. Always carry an important-looking document to maintain a façade of urgency, and have a simple query that only that person could answer as a way of legitimising the chat and the resulting time out.

FINAL THOUGHTS ...

Building a network takes time. Quite a lot of time. However, it is vital that you appreciate how important it is to be well-known and well-liked in your firm when you are starting out. Remember that knowing a lot of people is pointless if they all dislike you. To avoid this, take time to show you are interested in others, be enthusiastic about everything you do, do as much non-law stuff at work as you can justify/humanly manage, divorce yourself from any intellectual ego you might have and build a network with everyone who might have an impact on your career - no matter how small or insignificant that impact might appear. Combine this with the communication and commerciality skills we looked at in chapters four and five, and you will find that your brand builds very quickly and very positively indeed.

Conclusion

A FALSE DAWN?

You've been yawning through a long and boring presentation which – thank heavens – appears to be drawing to a close. Or so it seems, until you hear the speaker delivering the words, '*So, in summary, I would say …* ', followed by a 15-minute reiteration of what has already been covered, tagged with an '*Oh, and remember …* ' and a list of '*and one more thing*', not covered earlier on. That's when you know that the elation experienced earlier was, in presenting terms, a 'false dawn'.

You're frustrated and irritated, and think – rightly – that the presenter is guilty of poor planning and preparation.

Which is why the wrapping-up of this book avoids a 'false dawn' at all costs. In keeping with its mission to offer a simple and succinct 'how to', this conclusion is

- Brief

- Practical

- Free of any new, grand, drawn-out statements or any complex (or even simple) theories not covered earlier on

- Devoid of any attempt to tie everything together and thus risk undermining the practical nature of the material covered

It's a simple and final nudge towards the direction you should take in order to make a strongly positive impact as a junior commercial lawyer. Included in it is a list of actions for you to implement.

THE MODEL ...

It seems as though your challenge is to straddle the territory between being likeable but not wet, assertive but not arrogant, humorous but not silly and enthusiastic without appearing sycophantic. Essentially, it is about showing pride in your career choice, and a passion not for money but for business and how business affects the world around you.

Commercial lawyers (specifically solicitors) are specialist financial facilitators and sophisticated document producers. This is not to undermine the intellectual core at the heart of the profession and practice. However, if you appear to be just a pen-pusher and a document-production specialist without showing an aptitude and passion for business and the mechanics of finance, you won't make any real impression at all when you are starting out.

To maximise your impact in the early days when you might not know much about the work you are expected to do, the profession and/or firm in which you work, you might want to do the following:

- Ask **open questions** to show a genuine and proactive interest in the matter(s) on which you are working.

- **Seek appropriate feedback** and show those around you that you are implementing the feedback.

- **Laugh at yourself**; law firms are serious enough without you contributing.

- **Never show panic** - remember the image of the swan gliding gracefully through the water; its madly-paddling legs are out of sight.

- **Show enthusiasm** for whatever you do - even for tasks that are so boring they make you question the very reason for your existence.

- **Stay clear of gossip** - it never does anyone any favours. Ever.

- **Carve a niche for yourself** - if you are really interested in a specific topic or area, don't be afraid to communicate this to others.

- Never go anywhere without a **notepad and pen**, and always wear your smartest clothing when walking around your floor or meeting anyone you haven't met before. Be as smart as possible as much as possible.

- Always consider who it is you are communicating with and what they might need, want or demand before you enter the room or pick up the phone, always **tailoring your approach** accordingly.

- Make **face-to-face contact at work your default setting**, using the telephone as little as possible and thus building up a rapport with your recipient.

- **Follow-up** on every conversation and lead - send an e-mail confirming actions after every work-related conversation.

- **Never send an e-mail** or make a phone call when you feel **upset** or **angry**.

- **Never use the 'reply all' function** for e-mailing. Rather use the 'forward' function and manually type in all recipients.

- Don't be afraid to **ask for clarification** when ambushed by a senior colleague who delegates work to you in a rush. Remember, if you get it wrong because you did not ask questions at the time, you (and not the senior colleague) will be blamed.

- Always **ask for context** when receiving work: how does your piece of work fit into the jigsaw?

- **Ask to attend meetings** – no one will take you to them out of the goodness of their heart.

- Become a **master of process** - attain guru–Excel-spreadsheet status and offer your assistance to everyone who might need a spreadsheet.

- Deliver as many (interactive, well-prepared and researched) presentations and training sessions as you can. **High visibility** means positive brand.

- **Never deliver a presentation or a training session without understanding exactly what it is that the audience will take away at the end and why the business might need it.**

- **Avoid basic grammar mistakes** in any document - allow yourself to be criticised only for stylistic mistakes you couldn't have known about. And never make the same mistake twice.

- **Never under-promise or over-deliver.** Establish exactly what it is you're required to deliver and how you're expected to deliver it, and follow instructions. Thank whoever it is who has involved you and ask if your involvement can continue through the next stage.

- **Keep a tidy desk**; spend 10 minutes a day neatening things up, and never eat at your desk during work hours if you can help it. There is nothing worse than someone having to log in to your computer when you are away from your desk only to find three rancid peanuts, a grotty raisin and some crusty yoghurt under your keyboard.

WHAT'S THE 'RATIO' OF THIS BOOK?

Be human! It has been said that nice guys come last. That might be true for the Twenty-First-Century Solicitor 100m Sprint, when the rude, obnoxious and arrogant lawyers steam ahead simply through a mixture of aggression and audacity. But who wins the Twenty-First-Century Solicitor Marathon? No competition - it's the passionate, intelligent, likeable, approachable, good-humoured, robust, thoughtful, modestly-assertive, self-aware and enthusiastic professional who is most successful. He (or she, but let's stick to 'he' for brevity) is reliably punctual, turning up for meetings on time and ready to do business. He builds rapport if it is needed and is attentive to the answer when he asks how you are. He never seems to be under pressure (even when he is). He never misses deadlines, and always explains what he needs while listening to what others need in crunch situations. He appreciates the significance of business support functions in law firms, and shows appropriate interest and reliability in dealings with them. He – or shall we say 'you' now - also and crucially realises that there is more to life than work.

When you are starting out, you will probably have to accept that your family, social and romantic life might take a bit of a dent. But then you knew that when you decided to become a commercial lawyer … didn't you? Throw yourself in to your exciting new career in the right way, however, and you will make a positive, lasting impact on those around you at work and be rewarded accordingly in many ways. To achieve this, you will have to find the right twenty-first-century balance between lawyer and business person, speaking and shutting up, advising and listening, fun and serious, friend and colleague, and strategist and implementer, all the while enjoying every challenge that professional life throws at you with a smile on your face. You'll get there with a bit of hard work and an open mind.

Good luck!

AND FINALLY

A practical tip if you need a break …

Working as a commercial lawyer is stressful. If, after hours of intense work, you ever feel as though you need a break from your desk but worry that your more senior room-mate might wonder where you are, use the 'focus-rise-pause-scratch-mission' method to buy yourself at least 20 minutes:

FOCUS: This may be demonstrated by taking a legal-looking document, placing it on the desk space in front of you, turning away from your computer monitor and then examining the document closely by supporting your head in your hands on both sides like nothing else matters. Make sure your room-mate sees you do this so that he/she thinks you are 'in the zone'.

RISE: After at least 10 minutes of close examination, make a deliberate nod of the head and a soft, barely audible noise (eg, 'Hmmm') to display your considered and intellectual thought process. Then slowly rise to your feet, all the while examining the document intensely. This is to show tenacity and commitment.

PAUSE: Now walk towards the door holding the aforementioned document (still examining it intimately, but being careful not to bump into anything). When you get to the door, with your back facing your senior colleague, pause slowly and deliberately and narrow your eyes.

SCRATCH: To show you are really using your brain to think about this one, scratch your head and/or briefly hold your neck without moving, to display an earnest and thoughtful approach to your 'task'.

MISSION: Having shown that you are considered and thoughtful, it is time for action. Nodding and making a positive, purposeful noise, again barely audibly (eg 'Uh-huh'), walk off purposefully, holding your document.

Congratulations, you have now bought yourself 20 minutes to grab a coffee or some fresh air without worrying what your new room-mate might think.

When you arrive back at your desk, it's vital that you are carrying your original document plus something else (take something off the printer perhaps), and that you sit down quickly and decisively and launch straight into something on your monitor (eg drafting an email or another piece of work).

Good times...

Index

Lightning Source UK Ltd.
Milton Keynes UK
UKOW05f0851071016

284691UK00016B/252/P